MODERN FEAR THE INVISIBLE PRISON

A Powerful Invitation to Break Free From Fear

Leah Lovelight Michael

This book is designed for your inspiration and personal development. The author is not counseling, acting as a therapist, psychologist, or any mental health physician on the reader's behalf. Read this book with the understanding that you are fully responsible for your own choices, actions, and results. The stories represented are from the author's perspective and how she remembers and interprets the events and is not meant to cause harm. The author is not liable for how readers may choose to use this information.

Copyright © 2020 by Lovelight, LLC & Leah Lovelight Michael
All rights reserved. No part of this book may be reproduced or transmitted in any form or by any means, electronic or mechanical, without prior permission in writing from the author or publisher, except for the inclusion of brief quotations in a review.

Content Edited by Sara Roberts, CurioMethod
Grammar Edited by Erin Crabtree
Art Design: Nicholas Beuthien
Cover & Interior Design: Peak Marketing & Design
Photo Credit: Jenna Nord, Jenna Nord Photography, LLC
ISBN: 9798687753692

*This book is dedicated to the loving memory
of James L. Currier.*

*Dear Jimmy C.,
Your light will always be a guide for me.
In your passing, I found the connection to my purpose.
Forever grateful to you, dear friend, until our paths cross again.*

MODERN FEAR: THE INVISIBLE PRISON

The Many Veils of Fear

By Rachelle Niemann

Author of Breaking Free From the Hustle for Worthiness | www.rachelleniemann.com

Anger, sorrow, confusion, and chaos
You continue to outwit me
So determined and devious
So sure of my insecurity

I don't always recognize you
As you continue to adapt
Adopting new disguises
To keep holding me in your grip

You are my dis-ease
Courage is my antidote
I stand up and break free
But you creep back in with your unfamiliar identity

You kick me back down
Put me in my place
Maybe even deeper
Just in case

But I will not let you keep me here
I will seek you
Exposing your true face
And I will persevere

I will stand with courage
Again and again
I will fight with bravery
And eventually, love will win.

MODERN FEAR: THE INVISIBLE PRISON

CONTENTS

THE BEGINNING 1

FEAR 6

THE MIND 11

WHAT IS THE PURPOSE OF PRISON? 16

MODERN FEAR 20

SECTION 1 – RECOGNIZE 24

    Core Wound 26

    Past Lifestyle 35

    Prisoner of the Past 39

    Reliving the Old Story 42

    The Abuse Cycle - Trauma & Drama 45

    The Drain of Toxic People 55

    Anticipatory Anxiety 60

    When Anxious Turns to Reactive 64

    Procrastination 66

    The Four Letter Word - H*te 69

    The Mental Cell of Doubt 71

    Shame 73

    Suffering 76

    Money 77

    Chasing the American Dream 82

    The Shame of Scarceness 91

    The Pity Party 94

    Death 96

Judgemental Behaviors 98

Dishonesty 101

Selfish to Selfless 104

Self-Aware 107

Get to Know Your Bad Self 110

SECTION 2 – RECLAIM 114

Present Lifestyle - Reclaim Your Time 116

Social Lifestyle 122

The Influence of Your Environment 124

The Meaning of Truth is Relative 131

Faith 133

Relationships 135

Reclaiming Old Stories 137

Compromise 139

Contemplation 144

The Heart 150

The Formula 158

Forgiveness 161

Strong Enough 163

SECTION 3 – REWIRE 166

Intentional Lifestyle 168

Work and Lifestyle 171

Do You Repel Or Attract Money? 173

The Hope & Want of Desire 177

Dreams 180

Action 183

The House of Mirrors 185

Conscious Reality Creation 188

The Ebb and Flow 191

Clear Connection to Expectation 196

Owning the Power of Your Voice 200

Pause 204

Terrified Excited 207

From the Mind to the Heart 210

Connect with Nature 212

Never Try Never Know 215

SECTION 4 – RECEIVE 218

Remember You Already Know 220

Style Your Life 222

Giving & Receiving 226

What Purpose Does Love Serve? 229

Freedom of Internal Alignment 235

On the Path of Liberation 237

The Future 239

Love in Action Through Community 241

Do What Matters 243

Past, Present, Future 244

Choice 246

Acknowledgment & Appreciation 248

About Leah Lovelight 250

What Poeple Say About Working With Leah 251

MODERN FEAR: THE INVISIBLE PRISON

THE BEGINNING

*"Be miserable. Or motivate yourself.
Whatever has to be done, it's always your choice."
Wayne Dyer*

I spent years of my life in a victim mentality, blaming others, and protecting myself. I am no stranger to abuse: from others, from myself, and society. In my formative years, I developed a tough exterior, letting in very few people. I exuded false confidence trying not to appear weak, but it was an illusion. It was a developmental skill from growing up in a life of survival; blend in and do not draw attention. I developed so many masks; I was lost in the dishonesty of the stories I was living.

I cared about what people thought of me. I was afraid of their judgment. I compared myself to others and beat myself up when I felt insignificant. I was never satisfied with who I was.

I was imprisoned within myself. I was held captive by Modern Fear.

Modern Fear: the fear of feeling or being in a sovereign relationship with our feelings.

From a young child, I had a knowing that everything I experienced was for a purpose. I had to find meaning within my suffering. At times, I found it hard to make sense of my journey. Until recently, I was imprisoned by my own Modern Fear.

For the last few years, I have been living in Montana's secluded mountains, digging into myself, recognizing my barriers, reclaiming their hold on my energy, rewiring my intended purpose, and receiving from the universal power within myself.

After years of soul searching, I have learned that the traumas and dramas of life bring learning opportunities if you can move past the suffering. I reached a point in my journey where I became tired of listening to all of the anger, frustration, and exhaustion that filled the stories I was telling myself. I recognized I was asking the wrong questions. Instead of "why did this happen **to** me," I started asking, "why did this happen **for** me?"

I first started on my journey of writing this book years ago, thinking that I had a big idea that would change the world. I wanted to get my soul's message out of me, and I was in a hurry. I wanted to finish before my mentor, friend, and father figure, Jim, passed away. I desperately wanted his seal of approval on this book. I wanted to celebrate with him, and yet there was no hope. The message wasn't ready to be shared, and cancer took my friend too quickly.

With Jim's passing, the birthing of this book stopped. My heart broke open saying good-bye to him. I was trapped in my head, not wanting to feel my broken heart. I used the excuse of missing the "deadline" and walked away from the intention of sharing my message with the world. I first had to break free from my internal prison of Modern Fear.

Stepping away from writing, turned out to be a gift. I discovered so many more lessons within my own story. I learned that in order to heal, we must be willing to feel our wounds fully.

I had no choice but to go down the path of healing, which can often be extremely uncomfortable and confusing, with immense highs and lows. However, on the other side of fear is love.

I reflected on the meaning of my own life. I asked myself the question: **What matters most to me?**

Ironically, this question was difficult for me to answer because I was trying to live up to an unidentified expectation that I developed while listening to societal noise and feeling its pressure. I was under the belief that if I worked hard, I would be successful; however, I forgot to consider how I wanted to feel in life.

When I was striving to achieve societal success, I found my life in a state of dis-ease. I was under constant self-imposed stress, as I tried to attain a level of perfectionism that I know is not achievable.

The more I reflected on this idea of hard work, the more I recognized it was flawed. I realized my definition of success was blurred because there was no meaning behind it. By societal definition, I am "successful." I made the uphill journey from growing up in a drug-infested trailer park to "making it" in corporate America.

My idea of success has transformed from the approval of others to my own acceptance. I want to be in alignment with my values and feelings. If I am angry, I want to **feel** it. If I am happy, I want to feel it. I have become fascinated with how the state of our feelings contributes to the inner world of self and radiates to the outer world.

When we are in a state of dis-ease, we are uncomfortable. We do not have a sovereign relationship with our emotions, our mind is typically consumed with chaos, and our physical being might be showing signs of sickness. Most importantly, our energy is being taken from us or is being blocked by us.

Energy makes up everything in the universe and beyond, and as such, I believe that we are energy. When we are living in fear, our energy is constricted, and life can become challenging. Constricted or blocked energy moves us out of alignment, and we become more susceptible to the shadow frequency of scarcity. When we are living in love, our energy is in flow, and life is something we experience. When our energy is in flow, we become aligned with universal source energy, which allows us to tap into the naturally occurring abundance in life.

I spent years of my life in fear, with my energy constricted, living in a dis-ease state. Once I started my spiritual path and believed in something greater than myself, I finally felt love. Once I embodied love, I became love. Now I am here to serve love.

I am writing this book because I don't want people to suffer, trapped in fear. We can always follow our suffering back to fear. Fear is a constant. Love is a constant as well. Surprisingly, love can be harder to accept and sometimes receive until it isn't. This book is a roadmap for self-love if you are willing to accept your unconditional truth. No other can ever stand in the center of your truth, which makes it so sacred Good, bad, or ugly, all of my truths make up my reality, and the same is true for you.

I used to believe that my mind was where my truth resided. On my healing path, I discovered that my mind was actually the place that held me prisoner because fear originates from our mind. To truly liberate me, I had to go on a journey to discover the truth that resided within my heart. Only then was I able to discover my inner truths that I use to navigate my life.

Discovery of your inner truth will be an adventure on your path from your mind to your heart and is where you will experience sovereignty from Modern Fear.

This book is a guide for reclaiming lost power, rewiring your energy, and receiving your desired future.

It is a journey of breaking down the barriers of your invisible prisons and breaking through on life.

Planned or unplanned, being alive is a miracle. Life is a gift of experiences. Ebbing and flowing through expansion and contraction.

The quality of your life experience is a choice that you make every day. Believe it or not, you choose how you live your life, moment by moment. Yes, you have obligations that you may not like, but you have a choice on how to perceive those responsibilities. They can either drag you down or inspire you to grow.

Society's increasing disconnection from empathy and community is a warning sign that we need to open up our hearts and express our loving feelings, to reverse the dysfunction of the social slander that is wreaking havoc on our culture.

I believe a divide is coming.

There are going to be those who continue to allow themselves to be brainwashed by societal noise. They will look to television to escape reality, find relationships through "double taps," "swipes" and "likes," robotically participating in life with a desensitized approach to living. These people quest for external validation and will control their emotions through suppression. They will feel Modern Fear, reactive anxiety, and doubt, as they compare their lives to the public illusions presented by others who do the same thing.

Then there will be those who see the world is shifting. They will be observant of the decline of humanity. They will see the illusion of the falsely constructed reality that benefits the few at the cost of the many. They will revolt against mainstream societal expectations. These people will question their contribution to the world and will impact their own lives through self-discovery and acceptance for their journey. They will become beacons to humanity. These people will foster love, acceptance, hope, and will contribute to our emotional evolution. They are known as lightworkers.

Both types of people are necessary, and one is not better than the other. Their experiences are different. We all choose how we participate. I was once lost in the noise, escaping reality through mainstream entertainment and self-abusive habits. I was on the rollercoaster of societal acceptance, chasing a spoon-fed dream throughout my childhood by our culture. Then I mentally, emotionally, and physically broke because none of my life was for a purpose that originated within me. My life was being predetermined by what I thought was necessary to "succeed." This kept me trapped in survival mode and prevented me from thriving. During the process of rebuilding myself, I discovered the calmer, fulfilled sovereign quality of life encompassing liberation and enjoyment.

The journey this book offers is not for everyone. You will feel resistance as you contemplate your life and areas you might want to change. This resistance is fear, and it should be recognized because it is holding you prisoner. This book is challenging. Coming out of suffering requires reflective thinking. There have been many times during my journey out of Modern Fear that I've wanted to quit trying to "improve" myself because it was uncomfortable. There were moments that I thought, "forget it, I don't need to be a better person." I allowed myself to believe that I was fine, letting Modern Fear, anxiety, and doubt imprison me.

And yet, deep within my heart, I knew I needed to keep going not only for myself but for anyone else who is on the path of self-discovery out of fear.

In this book, we will learn to experience our own feelings deep from within our bodies and our soul. We will move through four sections:

- **RECOGNIZE** – To create change, we must first understand where we are.
- **RECLAIM** – Let go of the feelings that no longer serve our greater good, reclaiming the extended energy.
- **REWIRE** – Where we focus our intention and attention directly shapes our world.
- **RECEIVE** – Practice allowing the abundance of love to flow to you.

FEAR

"The cave you fear to enter holds the treasure you seek."
Joseph Campbell

The two most significant forces, what I call Evolutionary Frequencies, are Love and Fear. Both are connected to our survival and how we design our lives.

There is no one being or entity upon this earth that does not know the frequency of fear.

The instinctual feeling of fear has been with us since the beginning of time. It is an evolutionary feeling resulting in a reaction to a perceived threat of danger. It activates a fight, flight, or freeze response when survival is on the line. **This is healthy; fear is a helpful feeling; it saves lives!**

Fear is a frequency that can be felt more easily than love due to its distinct attachment to our survival. It can take away the ability to feel lighter feelings because it puts us into our primal brain responsible for survival, drive, and instinct. When we are in a constant state of fear or stress, it prevents or hinders the experience of leisurely feelings such as joy, peace, and love.

In my experience, Modern Fear induces the same reactionary stimulus and mimics the biological responses of the fight, flight, or freeze fear; however, our survival is not on the line.

Biologically the body cannot tell the difference between a perceived or real threat. The hormonal response to the stress of fear causes lasting effects. Even though we may not consciously feel the effects of the fear response, one still occurs.

I went to the doctor awhile back because I felt exhaustion, low motivation, and overall just knew I was off. My doctor decided to check my adrenals. I was shocked when I got the diagnosis of phase one adrenal failure. At the time of the diagnosis, I felt like life was stress-free; I was living in the country, with a healthy meditation practice, regular physical exercise, and a solid self-care routine. In my mind, I thought there was no reason for me to be stressed out; however, my body was physically producing diagnosable proof.

My doctor asked me to evaluate my lifestyle and see where I was overextending myself and where I could reclaim some of my energy. In this reflection process, I discovered that I hold high expectations for myself, especially regarding my job performance or working with others. These demanding expectations created subconscious stress, and as a result, my adrenal system became overworked and was failing. All of this was physically happening while I had no idea I was stressed out at all.

The relationship we have with Fear and Love directly controls our ability to feel, and we as humans are being manipulated and influenced to handle excessive amounts of fear.

I can say this with confidence because I recognize manipulation and the control it can have over us. When growing up in low socioeconomic status, everyone is trying to hustle someone else because there is too much scarcity. I have been manipulated, and I have been a manipulator, primarily because of having to be in survival mode, trying to get by. As we journey through this book, you will learn that it takes one to know one. If you think, "This person is doing this (fill in the blank)," I promise you, somewhere in your energetic field, you too are doing the same (fill in the blank). For example, if you feel you are being taken advantage of, then there is a likely chance that you may be crossing a boundary with other people and their generosity somewhere in your life.

I used to be emotionally numb to higher vibrational feelings like joy and love. I regularly battled with the **addiction to not being able to feel anything** other than the lower vibration of emotions such as shame, judgment, doubt, and worry. All of these feelings are connected to the fear frequency I was always on the search for the quick dopamine hits. This feeling was fleeting. My reactionary anxiety would get me mentally worked up, putting me into an active fear state. My thoughts became obsessive, and my body would experience a fear response, increased heart rate, and an overwhelming desire to run or hide.

My internal fear controlled every part of me, which would cause doubt, giving me an overwhelming desire to fade away and become invisible. I would move from a reactive fear state to a passive fear state, giving me a false illusion that fear was no longer in the driver seat; however, I was lost in the fear of doubting myself.

Doubting yourself and what you can accomplish destroys the feeling of hope. Doubting others and their intentions break down the ability to trust, resulting in fearing the repercussions from judgment and what might be used against you. This leads to a decreased ability and or desire to participate in life because these lower vibrations of existence bury the acts of appreciation or joy.

The behavioral fight, flight, or freeze response to fear creates emotional imprisonment within yourself.

Our ability to feel is exhausted because we are overstimulated by fear, which is what I refer to as **Modern Fear, the fear of feeling or being in a sovereign relationship with our feelings,** and I mean really feeling your own experience, in your body and in your soul.

It is our ability to feel that allows us to experience and know the vibrancy of life.

Modern Fear is still fear; however, it is not attached to our survival but to approval and acceptance from ourselves, often overshadowed by the need for external validation. As a result, Modern Fear can be found at the source of our reactionary anxiety and doubt.

We experience fear internally, and it is also essential to recognize the external forces of fear.

Fear is a frequency that is being used to control us through the manipulation of how our passive attention is being heavily influenced through screen time.

Culturally, we are experiencing an epidemic of fear. The brutality in mass media, entertainment, and consequential advertising has commercialized fear. Movies, television series, news, and media posts bombard our senses with rape, murder, drug use, relationship, and political drama; if evaluated, these themes should be discomforting. Yet the brainwash has taken hold. We don't experience these influences as a tragedy for humanity, but as entertainment for our lives.

As a result of Modern Fear, I look into the world, and I see zombies, not the zombies whose flesh is decaying, but the zombies whose souls are imprisoned and their lights are buried. This breaks my heart, and I am passionate about supporting others in breaking free of this invisible prison.

Today people are afraid to admit to having fear; it makes them feel weak and vulnerable.

Entertainment and the increasing connection to social media have smothered culture with the propaganda of fear. **The primal behavioral reaction to fear is being habituated and could ultimately lead to a societal demise.** At its essence, fear is meant to be a biological response that saves our lives, and now is something used to entertain us, our senses are being numbed. We now experience news reports where there are videos of bystanders recording crimes rather than calling the police or helping the victim. Even worse, we are now actually watching videos of police killing people in real-time, which is a brutality that is beyond the hands of justice.

Now, in addition to being scared and feeling fear by entertainment, the internet has created an alternative reality where anyone can share anything, whether it is true or not, which disrupts our ability to feel the security of trust. A new fear is being created, which I refer to as Modern Fear.

Is there something out there that is threatening your survival, or does it just **feel** like it?

Suicide is another epidemic we are facing culturally. There are too many of us dying by our own hands out of fear of the past or future. The threat to our survival could very easily be coming from within us. As a child, I thought of taking my own life when things felt too hard to keep trying. I felt defeated and hopeless. I have rationalized that the world would be better without me. I was susceptible to the belief that my life had no value and was tired of suffering from it.

I am grateful that I did not make a permanent decision of suicide for the temporary difficult times, even if the hardship lasted for years. If you feel like your life is being threatened by your own hands or by another, please, I urge you to seek support. The potential of suicide is devastatingly painful, and you are not alone.

Fear, which once supported humans as a survival response, is now holding us, prisoner, in judgment, anger, doubt, and reactive anxiety. This is not the way life has to be. There is an entire experience beyond fear that is waiting for you.

Take an active role and allow yourself to consciously feel again. Release yourself from the invisible prison of Modern Fear and take responsibility to engage with your fears so that they do not control you and rob you of life's fullness.

THE MIND

The mind; oh, what a beautiful gift, and how it has taken us to unknown territories. The mind holds our intellect, curiosity, and imagination. The mind resides within the brain, which is the ultimate processing center that has evolved us as humans. The brain itself has evolved, starting with our reptilian brain, or brain stem area, responsible for our survival and is where the fight or flight defenses originate. The brain later evolved to include the limbic system, which is located above the reptilian brain and is responsible for our emotional centers, which help to determine if we like something or not. The brain's final evolution is the addition of the neocortex, which gives us conscious awareness and allows for imaginations of the future and taking strategic action.

The mind allows us to see beyond the current reality and allows us to imagine and play with the idea of, "I wonder."

The world in which we live is a direct reflection of what the mind is able to achieve. For all the beauty the mind has created, it is also responsible for life's turmoil through greed, lust, and fear of death.

When we have an active relationship with our mind, we can harness the potential power of its ability to create. We can leverage that relationship to accomplish impossible things. When I was in my heavy lifting and Crossfit days, I held the mantra, "The mind controls the body." With dedicated discipline, I witnessed myself physically achieve tasks that still feel miraculous. I am a petite framed woman (at the time weighing in around 120 pounds), and my personal record for the back squat is 175 pounds, and the deadlift 220 pounds. In each of these accomplishments, I visualized every moment of the movement in my mind before my body ever touched the bar.

I had to believe to be able to achieve.

Professional athletes say the game is won in the mind before it is ever won on the field. A powerful mind or intellect can control pretty much anything.

As humans, our minds can be in an active state of consciousness or a subconscious passive state. For example, when we learn a new skill like driving, our mind is actively processing everything our eyes see, what our hands and feet are doing, and practicing anticipatory reaction to other unknown variables. When we first start driving, everything in our body is turned on. Then slowly, over months and years, as the physical behaviors become second nature, our mind becomes more passive when it is behind the wheel.

How often have you been driving, lost in dreamland, and suddenly become aware that you are driving and don't fully know where you are on the journey? I know that I am not the only one who has had this experience. The mind can become extremely passive; this is an evolutionary design to make life easier because its duty is to take our attention from a conscious state of being into a subconscious state of being.

Our mind is a superstructure that is so magnificent with its limitless potentials; however, it is also extraordinarily passive and wants to make life as easy as possible. Its primary function is to identify, categorize, and habituate.

There will be some of you who read this and are 100% okay with living a **passive mental lifestyle, unplugged from knowing that you are the creator of your reality**, and that is okay; however, you will absolutely remain trapped in Modern Fear. A passive mind is susceptible to influence, and your thoughts become a blend of the programming that has infiltrated your system mixed with your subconscious rationalization to them. For example, movie theaters are known to put subliminal messaging before the previews that subconsciously encourage you to go to the concession stand to make a purchase. Before you know it, every time you walk into the theater, you are programmed to go to the concessions and pick up some goodies before you even sit down.

Our susceptibility is significant to acknowledge if you want to break free from the prison of Modern Fear. **Feeling is an active state of being.** Our emotions are in motion and will quickly consume our physical body, and the mind will respond to make sense of them. If you practice becoming consciously aware of your feelings' physical nature, you will begin to build your subconscious response in a proactive rather than a reactive manner.

Our mind can create chaos, or it can influence with inspiration. Whatever our mind perceives, our reality will reflect. Some industries have taken advantage of the passiveness of the subconscious mind. Almost all major corporations, from banking systems to food manufacturers, know how to manipulate you and your mind through marketing, making you believe that life without their product is substandard.

Most of us are being brainwashed because we practice passive attention with our minds.

The programming that you watch, the music you listen to, and the people you hang around with all influence your mind, consciously or not.

I know that if I feel sad, I will turn on a tear-jerker of a movie. My mind is trying to rationalize my feelings by demonstrating that I am not alone in my sadness, and it is okay to be sad. Our feelings build and compound on themselves through internal stories and external influences. This is a compulsive and addictive tendency.

The mind is susceptible to influence, either through substance intoxication, the internal dramatic stories we create, or external manipulation. Our mind processes everything that happens in our lives from a state of constant stimulation and is therefore vulnerable to be programmed for addiction. These addictions can show up as chemical influence, behavioral tendency, compulsivity, or diminished control; workaholism, alcoholism, excessive exercise, compulsive gambling, sex, and lying can all be addiction types if they lead to impairment within one's life.

Our dramas, real-life or make-believe, program the addictive feelings to our personal stories, and it is easy to get caught up in these feelings. Our mind is the ultimate storyteller, which releases chemical responses within our bodies, and these chemical responses can become addictive. Dopamine and serotonin are love molecules, and at the beginning of new relationships, as our brain releases these neurotransmitters, our entire Being feels fantastic. We fall in love, which can become its own compulsive behavior.

Our mind also loves instant reward; like a lab rat searching for the cheese, our mind is an addict. It craves stimulus, good or bad. I was once addicted to self-abusive habits because that was the only way I could feel. I understood pain, anger, depression, and frustration because those intense reactionary feelings felt familiar and ordinary. Through my liberation, I now primarily feel joy, happiness, security, and love, so much so that now I am addicted to the feeling of love and self-care practices. Although most of us are all addicted to something, most of us are in denial or might feel shame around admitting it.

The mind can rationalize and bury our feelings as it becomes addicted to power and greed, which are hyper present in today's society. We can go from a passive mind into an over-controlling mind, where power, greed, and domination become a primary desire. The more controlling our mind, the less we tend to feel.

Then comes an addiction to control, where we try to manipulate our lives and others' lives. The need to control can strangle unknown opportunities, constricting our energetic field. The desire to control grows within Modern Fear as we try to use our mind to prevent feeling a certain way.

The mind craves power, it wants to be important, it seeks the vantage points, and **when trained correctly, the mind is one of our most valuable assets.**

Once you start to look around in life and see how your mind is being influenced and manipulated, you can interact with the collective reality differently.

Music theory is science. All music that streams to you through television programs and the radio is designed to bring you to a particular emotional state. Piano music, especially the lower cords, makes me emotional. This scale of music touches my soul, although I haven't always been aware of this influence. When I hear this type of music, emotions swell within me, my throat constricts, my thoughts go to sad memories, and I cry as the music takes me over, and my heart breaks wide open. This physical response happens because this music is designed to initiate these types of feelings. I could be perfectly happy, hear this music, and become sad. I had no boundaries to this mental and emotional influence.

Then I developed a conscious practice with my feelings and how they are being influenced. Whenever I notice a change in my feelings, I ask, "Is this mine or is it yours?" We will discuss this tool in more detail later in the book.

If the feelings are genuinely mine, they will remain present even with conscious awareness. If I am experiencing a feeling because of an external influence, like music or someone else's bad mood, when I ask the question, "Is this mine or is it yours?" the feeling subsides because I am shifting the subconscious influence into a conscious state of awareness.

Being aware of how your mind is influenced is a practice that will support a healthier relationship with your feelings. The tool of objective witnessing, like questioning "is this mine or is this yours," is an excellent practice for your mind and provides an opportunity to reclaim your energetic power from influences that you may have not even been aware of before.

Our intellect is a tool that needs to be used and explored. If you are too passive, you can be lost in the noise. If you are too controlling, you can be lost within your own self.

Remember, our mind is the source of our thoughts, which will translate into words, and the words we use will create the world in which we live.

Our mind is powerful. Honor and respect it and make sure not to follow it blindly.

You become the designer of your life by having an active relationship with your mind and thoughts. Throughout this book, we will explore how our minds are influenced and influence us in subconscious programmed patterns. More importantly, we will develop tools that will allow us to create our reality consciously.

WHAT IS THE PURPOSE OF PRISON?

"Your perspective on life comes from the cage you were held captive in."
Shannon L. Alder

The invisible prison of Modern Fear protects or hides pieces of yourself that make you feel vulnerable. Most experiences that we are afraid to feel are painful; they hold shame, judgment, and thus make us feel weak. So we build a prison around these experiences to keep them secret or hidden. We defend ourselves from the potential of heavier feelings, which tend to bring up areas of vulnerability.

Suppressing vulnerable experiences of feelings gives strength to Modern Fear. As these fears are buried within us, they can become reactive triggers, landmines waiting to explode.

I feel most vulnerable when it comes to betrayal and find it confusing to have my trust broken. I have experienced betrayal by others, such as when my boyfriend and best friend slept together. I have experienced betrayal by myself, like when I withhold sharing my feelings because I am afraid of hurting someone else. We are all vulnerable to betrayal.

We are all sensitive to our vulnerability. When used against us, we retreat further into Modern Fear. Protection from others is a natural reflex; we hideaway to remain safe from risking our tender feelings. Fear of manipulation controls this behavior of holding back.

Feeling vulnerable is a raw experience. Blaming others for our pain is easier than accepting our contribution to our triggered vulnerability.

When I feel vulnerable and betrayed, I can run through a broad spectrum of emotions. With the first shock, I find myself seeking clarity and asking why? I then quickly move into anger, and my ideas of revenge can get pretty creative. Sadness follows the anger; I don't believe people genuinely want to hurt each other, and I most certainly fear to hurt others. I then move into more of a solution-based thinking process, such as how can I communicate that I am hurt? How can I remain open to the fact the other person might not care or even know? It is even worth sharing my pain with the other person, and do they want to grow with me? Where can I hold myself responsible for my feelings? Is this something that I can process within me? Eventually, I move into an acceptance of the experience and find forgiveness, which is how we are liberated from the Modern Fear of vulnerability.

Communication is a vulnerable experience, and holding back your voice will keep you trapped within the prison of Modern Fear. I know that personally before I can find the courage to use my words to express my hurt feelings, I often have revisited the vulnerable experience so many times that the story can become one-sided to my vulnerable perspective. As a result, the pain is magnified. If I have become too lost in the pain, then by the time I share my feelings, the other party can feel like I am blaming or attacking them.

What would it take to share our vulnerable feelings with the intention of healing rather than harming?

The story that you are telling yourself right now determines the feeling that you are having at this moment.

The prison of Modern Fear has many cells, unlock one, and you'll discover another. It is an unknown adventure. During the journey, you are bound to face memories, ideas, and beliefs that will challenge you and your desire to release Modern Fear. Being numb is a response to protect our vulnerability; while it can appear to be more comfortable, it is much less fulfilling.

I judge myself more harshly than anyone else. I am my own worst critic. This inner, judging critic, also known as my perfectionist, is one of the contractors of my prison of Modern Fear. Perfectionism protects the vulnerable feeling of failure.

My doubts, my reactive anxiety, my shame are all my cells of Modern Fear. These feeling states offer opportunities for me to learn to have a healthier relationship with them, so that I may open the doors to the cells of my invisible prisons.

How badly do you want to find yourself? Through each cell you enter, each truth you discover, you will find a small piece of yourself hidden, and it is then your choice to liberate that part of you and to reclaim the energy that was once blocked.

Imagine each cell within your prison as having stored potential energy that is trapped behind the door of an energy block like shame or reactive anxiety. As we learn to be with these types of reactionary feelings rather than rejecting them or allowing them to overtake us, the energy block is loosened, swinging open the prison cell door. As the imprisoned potential energy is released, you can viscerally process a once buried experience on the somatic level. As these blocked, draining energies are released, we reclaim parts of ourselves that no longer need to be hidden. As a result, we are empowering our relationship with ourselves.

There will be prison cells where the feelings of hopelessness, sadness, anger, frustration, and doubt will feel too great to bear. Discovering hidden truths can be painful, and this pain can be a deterrent for wanting to open up each respective cell. On the road to freedom, there are going to be points that you will want to stop, or worse, turn around to old belief structures. You will need to choose if you sincerely want to open up. It can feel like there is no escape, but that is not necessarily true. Instead, it may indicate that you are not yet ready.

Be kind to yourself if you come upon a cell that is not ready to be released. Allow it to be, as we cannot force reclaiming. This is a journey where we learn to be compassionate to ourselves. The parts of ourselves that live in our shadow are not used to receiving love, they are not used to being cared for, and it takes time to build trust within your own being. The path of shadow work, or working with the sides of ourselves that have been hidden or we have kept hidden, requires perseverance, dedication, discipline, and above all, kindness, compassion, and forgiveness. Be truthful and vulnerable with your feelings, allow them to flow and escape their prison, and reclaim that energy.

If we release energy without the intention of reclaiming the healing energy back within our self, we create a void within our energetic field. When you release, what do you want to attract? There have been many mornings after a night out where I would wake up, shaming myself,

18 | MODERN FEAR: THE INVISIBLE PRISON

and then make the statement, "I am never going to drink again." This was a false promise, which caused my energetic field to attract more opportunities to learn my lesson. When I finally quit drinking, I did not promise myself that I would never drink again. Instead, I committed that I was never going to be that toxic person again. I reclaimed the power from the part of myself that liked to self-sabotage and disrespect myself. Inside, I allowed a new self that honored my oath to be a better version of myself.

Reclaiming and rewiring energy can be hard work. Throughout this book, I will share tools that I have used to support myself through this process. Repeat offenses of old behaviors, thoughts, and feelings will reoccur as we consciously put efforts towards change. Expression of reactive anxiety and doubt are habits that you practice over and over again, until one day you do not.

To find your freedom, recognize your habits, and listen for your truths.

Once a triggering truth comes to the surface, support that feeling, figure out if it is the Modern Fear source, or only a spark to initiate the change. Repeat, repeat, repeat.

Reclaiming is a practice of curiosity and contemplation. You can ask the same types of discovery questions to yourself over many years and get different answers because you are always changing.

Each moment you are a different person influenced and inspired by what has happened throughout your life's journey. You will know when you have come to the freeing answer, like tipping over the first domino, everything falls in line. You will experience relief and an enormous amount of acceptance in your life. The once constructed prison will no longer be there to block your energy. This newly available energy will help create the life you desire.

MODERN FEAR

Modern Fear: the fear of feeling or being in a sovereign relationship with our feelings.

Modern Fear is not a sudden response. It is the consequence of many decisions and life experiences pivoting around you and your choices that slowly debilitate your ability to feel.

Modern Fear builds and impacts your life when your thoughts, feelings, and actions are out of equilibrium with your core values, which are your fundamental beliefs that dictate behaviors between "right" and "wrong."

Your core values and my core values might not be the same. What we value is entirely subjective to our personal experiences.

If you have never taken the opportunity to explore your core values, I will invite you to stop and take a moment to feel for three or four driving forces within your life. These values may change over time and what you are experiencing.

Right now, my top three core values are:

- I value security, and money is a primary contributor to security. As such, I have an incredibly intimate relationship with my spending and savings.
- I value honesty, and even though telling the truth sometimes can feel like dying, this is the most powerful way to build trust and stability.
- I value deep, meaningful, unconditional connection, where I know it is safe to open my soul and shine in all parts of myself.

If I find myself stressed out about money, or I hear myself or someone else being dishonest, or I am not able to engage with others entirely, I will notice a resistance within myself. This awareness helps me be more attuned when Modern Fear has returned to my reality. Subtle conflicts will arise, and slowly I begin to experience constrictions in my life as I withdraw in an attempt to hide from the fear that is building.

When we are in fear and survival mode due to insecurities, our negative beliefs can impact our core values. Our core belief might reflect:

- A belief that life is a path of hardships and only the strong survive.
- A belief that we cannot change anything and that we are powerless.
- A belief that people can't be trusted and everyone is out for personal gain and is threatening.

If you fall victim to negative beliefs, your energetic field can become suppressed by pressure, stress, fatigue, worry, anxiety, and restlessness. This state of being, makes it more difficult to find appreciation and prevents us from fully allowing happiness and peace into our lives.

Limiting beliefs, which is being in a state of contracted energy or shutting yourself off from feeling, are consequences of Modern Fear. The dialogue of your thoughts will deteriorate. Negative self-talk will affirm ideas like:

- "I am too tired."
- "I don't have time."
- "I can't."
- "I won't."
- "I shouldn't."
- "I need approval."
- "I am not worthy."
- "I do not deserve."
- "I am insignificant."
- "I am not valuable."
- "There is something wrong with me."
- "I have issues."
- "I don't want to live."

At first, these statements can be quiet. You might already be saying them, and you are not consciously aware of the inner conversation. The festering happens as you try to avoid heavier feelings as they are overwhelming.

Unless you practice active listening, there can come a time when these limiting statements might dominate your self-talk, mostly if left unchecked.

Your thoughts will imprison you. I can openly share that in trying to create this book, it was incredibly difficult to feel all my feelings connected to my old story, and my self-doubt lead to negative self-talk. I had to consciously be in compassionate conversation with myself to prevent getting lost in the misery of old stories.

What is your relationship with your self-talk? Read through the list of limiting beliefs and notice which ones feel most personal to you. We all say these statements. Get curious here, and for the next 24 hours, challenge yourself to listen to how you speak inside your head and out loud. What are you saying? How do your words make you feel?

The law of attraction = Like attracts Like
Negative magnetizes negative.
Positive magnetizes positive.

Through the law of attraction, Modern Fear effects are exponential and build upon each other. For example, maybe you work with a bully that makes you feel intimidated at first, so you shy away from being confrontational. This holding back of your feelings gives this bully even more of a foothold, and their behavior continues until one day you blow up and react in an angry confrontation. Now everyone's feelings are hurt, and both parties are blaming each other for the discord. Before you know it, both of you are holding back reactive emotions that are trapping you in Modern Fear due to fear around the consequences of expressing your feelings, which buries your feelings even further.

In the same situation above, imagine if you could have a conversation with that bully, allowing each other to share perspectives, allowing for forgiveness. You share that their behaviors are hurtful, and in your experience, you know that a hurtful person is in a lot of pain and that instead of reacting to their negativity, you held a space for them to share their discomfort. This is an example of emotional intelligence, which begins with being able to observe our own feelings and the impact they can make. Their pain is not your pain, and their behaviors do not get to dictate your actions.

Imagine how wonderful life could be if we communicated our beliefs with open minds and open hearts? You will know that you have found a reliable escape from Modern Fear when you can connect into your core values and align with your internal beliefs rather than getting trapped in the limiting conversations we can have with ourselves and others.

SECTION 1

RECOGNIZE

*To acknowledge formally or
take notice in some definitive way.*

*"The reason a lot of people do not recognize
opportunity is because it usually goes around
wearing overalls looking like hard work."*
Thomas A. Edison

In this section, we will explore the "darker" side of our feelings.

Fear takes hold of us because our safety, security, or stability is being threatened.

It is essential to recognize what your current relationship with fear is.
Do you avoid it?
Do you love it?
Do you ignore it?
How is fear present in your life?

This part of the book's journey is triggering. There is no other way to warn against this section of the book gently. I openly share my uncomfortable, imprisoning experiences. I offer the challenges I have faced as an opportunity for you to explore your own experiences.

To release what no longer serves, we must first become aware of the effects these uncomfortable feelings have on us now.

The practice of consciously recognizing fear and its effects is a primary tool for releasing yourself from Modern Fear. We must become comfortable with observing the uncomfortable to stand witness for the life we want to live.

CORE WOUND

I feel that it is primarily our family units that can wound us the most. Family is meant to be there to protect and support us as we learn to become good humans. Our parents are responsible for programming us to be respectful contributors to society. They are meant to influence us morally and inspire us to grow.

Parents lay the foundation for our psychological and physiological safety, providing us with a safe home and an environment that allows us to learn from our mistakes and grow into healthy adults. When these securities are not met in our youth, we can become physically, emotionally, mentally, or spiritually wounded.

I am not villainizing parents here, as no manual says this is what it takes to be a good parent. To raise a human seems like the most challenging thing a person could do. Children reflect everything to us. They show us how we inspire them by lighting up, and they show us how we have failed them by breaking down. To be a parent is to move through a looking glass of our lives, with all of our being exposed's flaws and beauty.

My mother lived in Kansas, and my father lived in Montana. They met via a singles ad in the back of a magazine, and my mother made the journey to Rock Creek, Montana, where my dad's family ranch had been for some time. During this week-long rendezvous, my soul decided these two people would be my parents.

When it was discovered that my mother was pregnant, my parents tried to give it a shot. My mother and two older siblings moved to the Montana ranch to live with my father. The relationship between my mother and father did not work out, and while she was still pregnant, all three returned to Kansas, and I was born to a single mother. A few years later, my youngest brother was born, and thus my mother had four mouths to feed.

As a single parent, my mom hustled to provide for her family. I can't remember a time that my mom didn't work; she was often gone, so my older sister assumed more of a parenting role. From a young age, we all shared the responsibility of running a household; we all cooked, cleaned, grocery shopped, and cared for each other. Even with my mom always working, it was hard to make ends meet. We received financial assistance from the government and food stamps. We were part of the Mormon congregation and often received assistance through Deseret Industries for food or money from the bishop to help pay rent. We would often bounce from place to place following the financial support of the men my mom would meet.

My oldest sister was hit by a car when I was pretty young. She was seriously injured and hospitalized. As a single mom, this was a considerable weight to carry, and my sister shared with me that my mom was considering putting myself and my younger brother up for adoption because she simply didn't know how to manage the financial burden. At the time, I had an extremely close relationship with a family from the church. Doris and Jim, and their daughter Lori, lived in Kansas's open plains, where they had a big home and were secure. I would often spend the weekend at their place. Doris sold Avon, and Jim was a farmer who raised fighting roosters; as a family, they ate dinner around the table, and we played games all the time. I was delighted to be with them, and I always felt safe. Had my mother given me up, this is where I would have ended up. When I was younger, there were many times that I wished this would have been my fate, and yet now, as an adult, I am grateful it wasn't.

Frustrations and short tempers were common in our home. The count of three meant something. Whatever the request was, if three was reached, there was going to be physical punishment. My mother used this parenting method, and when my older siblings were in charge, they too harnessed the power of fear. Of course, later in life, when I was in charge of my younger brother, I would mimic the same behaviors. The worst "punishment" I ever received was with a vacuum cord; my mom swung that cord until she couldn't swing anymore. By then, I had built up a tolerance to physical punishment, and I can still remember receiving those stinging, flesh welting strikes, and in my head saying, don't cry, don't give that to her.

I have very few actual memories of my early years. I spent most of my formative life disassociated from my sensory experiences, sense of self, and personal history. When I first started on my healing journey, it was these suppressed memories that I was seeking. I felt like I was broken because I could not remember my life, and if only I could remember, then maybe I could be fixed.

My dad was a countryman, living the majority of his life six miles up the valley road of Rock Creek. Around eight years old was the first time I met him after my family decided to leave Kansas and move to Montana. I can still remember the nervous feeling in my stomach, wondering whether or not my dad would like me. He was a bowler, and the plan was to meet him at Westside Lanes bowling alley. I clung to my mom, twitching around as we walked inside, questioning her, "What I am supposed to call him?"

She replied, "Ask him."

Inside the bowling alley, she pointed him out before we approached him. He was a huge man, tall and wide, with red hair and blue eyes. He was wearing these brown polyester pants and a button-up short sleeve shirt. He had a heavy breath to him, and I am confident this was because of the labor his body endured by carrying around the extra weight. The conversation was pretty superficial, and I can imagine he was more nervous than I was, meeting his firstborn child for the first time. After a few minutes, I finally worked up the courage. I was hanging on the edge of a counter, bracing myself, and turning to look right up at him, I asked, "So what am I supposed to call you?"

He looked down at me and said, "You can call me anything you want, except late for lunch." This answer didn't support me at that time. It only made me feel more awkward. Today, it brings a smile to my face.

My father was a simple man, and he was married to a woman who was threatened by me. She made sure our relationship was limited. I saw my dad and his daughter, my younger sister, at the bowling alley on league night. We would play video games, and I would get to eat grilled cheese sandwiches from the deli. On rare occasions, I would go out to his home and spend time exploring the Sapphire Mountains and playing outside.

When we left Montana and moved to Florida, my dad would write to me from time to time; however, the relationship dwindled. Out of sight, out of mind.

I was my mother's only child who got to have a relationship with their father. We each had different dads, and I always felt grateful that I got to know him, even if he wasn't entirely in my life.

As an adult, when my partner and I moved to Rock Creek, one mile up the road from my dad's property, my reality around my father shifted. I would drive past where he had lived almost his entire life, and I would imagine what I would be like if I had grown up there. The community of Rock Creek has a lot of old-timers that have lived up in these mountains for years, and most people knew my dad.

As I met community members, the question was always asked, "What brought you here?" I got to share my story, and I would include my father. The look of shock from people when they would hear Rock Creek Red was my dad made me realize that he never talked about me, and no one knew I existed.

At first, I was confused: wasn't my dad proud of me? I wondered why he never made me part of his life. Maybe he was ashamed of me. Perhaps he was ashamed of himself. My father abandoned me and chose to live his life like I didn't exist. Am I not worthy of a father's love? Even writing these questions, it is hard not to feel sorry for me. If I had a father, maybe I wouldn't have been violated by so many men. If I had a father, perhaps I would have lived a more secure life.

As I was trying to make sense of the feelings of abandonment, I decided to read the letters my dad had sent to me while I was living away from Montana. What I found was a lot of pain. Every letter talked about the physical pain of his life. I also found scarcity, as every letter shared how hard it was to make ends meet. I also found a tenderness from an old countryman doing the best he could trying to be a father to a little girl he didn't know.

Recently, I visited my father at a nursing home. His body can no longer support his weight, and he isn't able to fully care for himself. His daughter had made some posts about his health on Facebook, and I realized that I might not have another chance to tell my father how I felt.

While preparing to see him for the first time in many years, many scenarios ran through my head of how the connection or conversation would go. My dear friend Katrina picked me up at the Seattle airport, and we went straight to the nursing facility. In my mind, I was preparing to say good-bye to a dying father.

When I walked into the room, rounding the privacy curtain, I witnessed my father see and recognize me. At that moment, I received the acknowledgment that my heart needed from my father, who couldn't be there for me as his daughter. He hadn't forgotten about me. He knew exactly who I was.

The conversation shared was about food; he wanted sweet and sour pork, and Katrina set out to make that happen. I shared with him that Rock Creek truly feels like home, and I am grateful it is where I have planted my roots. He asked if I had met some of his old friends and shared some gossipy stories.

I asked him if he had a belief for what happens when we pass away.

"Well, I guess I have never really thought about it. I sure hope there is bowling. I would hate to end up in a coal mine," he responded. "I know that I will be buried with my animals under the apple tree."

Katrina returned with the sweet and sour pork. All of my dad's attention shifted to getting that goodness into his stomach. As I prepared to leave, standing at the edge of his bed, I looked into his eyes, which was like looking into my own, and I said, "I don't know if I am going to be seeing you again. I want to thank you for my life and the part you had in creating me."

"It was sure great that you stopped by," he said as he shoveled another bite of sweet and sour pork into his mouth and lifted his hand to wave me good-bye.

Without hugging my father, I walked out of the room, understanding that my dad is not a deep man. He lived a simple life that was filled with hardships. He has his burdens to carry and didn't need my anger or guilt for his decision not to be part of my life. I recognized that I had amplified my feelings of being abandoned by all the stories I had been making up about him.

I genuinely hope that the end of life for my father is one that takes him gently into the night. Someday, I will go for a mile walk down the road to where my father's ashes will be buried underneath the apple tree. I will be able to sit next to his resting spot, and I will give my full sadness over to this apple tree, letting it absorb my tears as I cry for all children that have to grow up without one of their parents. I will lay my heart to rest with full acceptance of my father's journey, allowing forgiveness to grow as deep as the tree's roots.

I believe that most of our core wounds come from the betrayal of our safety during childhood like abuse or growing up without two parents; however, that is not always true. We are human. Our feelings can always be wounded.

During my very first Reiki attunement, I experienced an extraordinary world. I found myself floating freely in what felt like a lake or an abyss. From my internal perspective, I looked up to see these massive mountains with deep crevasses, all leading to a body of water. Then my experience was rotated 180 degrees, and I realized that I was within my mother's womb, floating in amniotic fluid. These were not deep mountainous crevasses; they were the veins and arteries of the placenta, nourishing my well-being. With a rushing feeling, I was transported from the comforts of the darkness and cast into the world's light. I recall being given to my mother. I could see her sweat-soaked hair stuck to the brow of her head. I could feel myself cradled in her arms. I saw her hand reaching to pull the blanket away from my chin. I remember seeing my mom's eyes look deep into mine, and hers filled with tears as she said, "I love you."

I have resisted this statement my full life, even though I know it is true. My mother has always unconditionally loved me, even to a fault at times. My mother played favorites with her children, and I was on top a lot. This type of favoritism was hard because it isolated me from my siblings, it made me a point of comparison, and it made me not want my mother's love.

Every single one of us starts the journey in the same way. We are created by an egg and a sperm, completing their single purpose – to create a life. We are formed through countless divisions of our cells in rapid biological magic, until we are a fetus, living our life floating through the abyss with everything we need already inside of us and where everything we need is provided to us.

Then we die. That free-floating abyss way of life is left behind, as we make our way through an extremely dramatic and contracting experience of birth. Think about it: every time our mother's womb contracted, it was by far the scariest experience that we cannot consciously remember. We start our journey as a creature that can live and breathe in fluid, we get repeatedly crushed over and over again as we make our way through a dark tunnel, and then suddenly we are air-breathing land creatures blinded by the bright light.

Talk about having your understanding of reality turned upside down and not fully comprehending why this happened. Talk about an ultimate betrayal, the womb's environment that once protected and supported us is stripped away, and we are cast out into the world to be something completely different.

Birth is our first death in this lifetime, devastation, and creation happening simultaneously. I am guessing that most of us are not going to remember this core wound. Our bodies and our minds have the best defense mechanisms of subconscious forgetting, protecting us from trauma. As we learn to explore our core wounds, we get to practice being an archeologist, excavating the tender layers with kindness, compassion, honesty, and forgiveness.

My core wounds were buried, subconsciously seeding a belief that love is dangerous, trust is fragile, and worthiness must be earned. To this day, I am still completely fascinated when I see a family that is bonded together and wonder, what made this dynamic work for them? I can become triggered when I see others who are supported and loved by their parents. I get sad that I prevent myself from allowing a relationship with my mother. I get angry at myself for still harboring aggressive feelings towards her.

The past has happened, and there is no changing it. I am triggered by the resistance I have for not allowing space for the bigger version of myself to come forth and truly forgive, not my parents, but forgive myself for how I continue to hold back my love from them. I am punishing them and myself. I am human.

Recognizing my core wounds of betrayal and abandonment has allowed me to explore my resistance and Modern Fear to feeling love. I was afraid of love because the experience of receiving love from my parents came with a cost. I couldn't trust love, so I blocked receiving it.

In learning to recognize the triggers attached to my core wounds, I began to heal my relationship to love. Releasing myself from the solitary confinement of Modern Fear, where I believed that I was not worthy of feeling love. The exploration of our core wounds is not an easy path to explore, and it might not be one that you want to do on your own. It is hard work, and I know the support and guidance I received while excavating these traumas was necessary for me to feel safe enough to release my heartbreak.

The opportunities to overcome adversity, most of which originates from my youth, shaped my spiritual path while breaking free of Modern Fear and reclaiming my ability to feel.

As we move through our experiences that keep us buried in Modern Fear, we start with our immediate field. As the layers go more in-depth, so do the lessons and the healing. There may come the point where you find a core wound that you don't want to be real. These are the ones that we will fight with the most resistance.

I am still in the process of exploring my core wounds from my upbringing, and this is okay. I am still reclaiming the wholeness of my energy from my family. I will tell you right now; you will never wake up one day and be fixed. The truth is, one day, you will wake up and recognize that you are not broken.

I recently learned about a practice within Japanese pottery called Kintsugi or golden joinery. In this practice, rather than discarding a broken bowl, they mend the bowl with golden lacquer. This philosophical perspective treats breakage and repair as part of an object's history, rather than something to disguise.

This imagery creates such beauty for me as I embody the knowing that I am not broken. As I recognize the deep wounds and triggers of my life, I practice reclaiming the energy and now imagine my own being a pottery piece that I am mending with liquid gold. Reclaiming energy that was once anchored in old wounds is a process. The more wounds that are healed with golden energy, the less the weight of the resistance we will feel. It is a practice that we get to do every single day, bit by bit, moment by moment.

I promise you, what we resist will persist, and what we accept will flow.

PAST LIFESTYLE

Past social class and family dynamics will significantly influence our present and future lifestyle, which is built by our habits, beliefs, and values. As you grew up, your parents' lifestyle lay the foundation for the lifestyle that you subconsciously identify with, whether you liked that lifestyle or not.

The deck is stacked against single parents. As a single mom, my mother was supposed to provide for all of us financially, emotionally, physically, and spiritually. This is a tall order for any one person to take on, as it is too much responsibility. In reality, maybe my mom shouldn't have had children because the burden was too great. I am undoubtedly grateful this was not her reality because I wouldn't be here. As a single parent, living in an impoverished socioeconomic class, my mom had to work all angles, and she did, grasping for anything that felt like it could be an anchor for stability.

I lived a life of habituated fear as I watched my mom struggle, witnessing her worry about how to feed us and to keep a roof over our heads, and I also observed her journey of trying to find love in her life. I knew we lived in scarcity. Watching my mom try to survive was both terrifying and complicated to experience.

We were always on the move. I was born in Kansas, and then we moved to Montana, then Florida, then Utah and back to Montana. We moved wherever my mom could find support, which wasn't always positive. I know my mother did the best she was capable of; however, I was aware that our basic survival needs put a strain on life. She didn't always make the best decisions. There are many people out there who are willing to do bad things that don't appear to be evil at first.

In the summer of seventh grade, my mother, younger brother, and I became homeless. My aunt took me, and my mother and younger brother attempted to find a way to make it on their own. My mother met this truck driver named Yogi. He promised a better life for my mom, and as a family, we moved from Utah back to Montana. Yogi provided shelter and financial security for us, and he was a predator. He wasn't around too often because he was a long-haul driver, but his attention focused on me when he was. He would come into my room late at night, telling me how much he loved me, pulling me close as he would kiss me with his Heineken-soaked breath. I was so angry at my mother for once again exposing her children to abuse. Home wasn't safe, and neither were new people.

One day, my mom asked me to do the dishes, and I blew up at her. At the end of the argument, she told me that if I didn't want to live by her rules, I could leave, and she kicked me out of the house. I went to live with the family of my best friend at the time. From my perspective, the Sturgis' had everything. They were a whole family unit; mom and dad were married, they had a safe home, and the pantry was full of food. I remember being impressed that Laura even received money for doing chores. The months I spent in that home saved me from how far things could have gone with Yogi.

I learned to be a chameleon and to fit in wherever we landed. As an empath, it was incredibly easy to take on the energy of those around me. As a survival technique, I spent my youth observing others so that I could figure out how to be accepted. I had an internal desire to fit in as a form of protection to prevent unwanted attention. I wanted to be loved, yet I didn't trust love. I took on a tough exterior, and the harder I became, the easier the uprooting of my life became. I built a prison around myself to protect myself from the fear of my life.

Breaking the hold and releasing the identity of scarcity was one of the most challenging shifts in beliefs that I have had to face. Within my experience of scarcity and poverty, there is not enough, and that is a fact. Resources like money and food are limited. I remember one time when I was pretty young, maybe like second grade, I ordered a pizza without asking my mom's permission. When the pizza arrived, I played dumb and denied ordering a half pineapple, half pepperoni pizza. I can still hear my mom and her tone when she looked at me and said, "I really didn't have the money for this." Within scarcity, one person's wants takes away from another person's resources. I felt so guilty at that moment when I realized the ten-dollar pizza was a big deal to our family and that I had put my selfish desires of hunger above my family, even though I had ordered the family favorite.

Even as a fully secure adult, I often felt like a fraud. I didn't trust money, and yet I had made my way into the money world. I worked for a brokerage firm with high net worth customers. For the first time, I experienced the way the "rich" lived. During the client appreciation parties, everyone would dress-up, and there would be catered food and open bars. I would find myself speaking with executives and leaders who were impressive to me. On the exterior, I was putting on my chameleon mask, but I was in fear on the inside. What if I said a word wrong? What if I was using inappropriate manners (what the heck are manners anyway)? What if they discovered who I really was? At my core, I lived imprisoned by the identity of being a poor little girl from a trailer park. My worthiness has always been a trigger for me. I struggled to value my worth because I projected that people somehow knew my past and felt pity for me, which made me feel shameful.

We are all unique individuals. When we compare ourselves to others, we are setting an impossible standard. When we strive to be like someone else, look the way they do, act the way they do, or achieve what they have achieved, we are ignoring our genius. We can become lost in the feeling of never being good enough because we are never allowing ourselves to be ourselves. There is no one else like you, and no one else can ever fully understand the effects of your juvenile lifestyle other than you. As I learned to harvest the golden lessons from my youth, I found appreciation for my past. Because of my unique history, I know that I can fit in anywhere from the barroom to the boardroom. People will always make assumptions about me, but they will only ever know for sure should I choose to share my truth with them. You are the one that knows you best.

Most parents do care and want to do what they believe is right, even when their best does not appear to be good enough. In this knowing, I have been able to find forgiveness towards my parents. We are all human and are giving this complicated thing called Life our best efforts. You might have been raised needing something: food, shelter, love, or connection. Or you might have been raised with abundance, never wanting for material items, but needing opportunity for failure, so that you could learn conflict resolution. I witness many parents doing everything for their children, which prevents their youth from learning basic life skills and emotional well-being during uncomfortable or complicated situations.

Some pasts might appear to have more hardships than others, but adversity is a relative position and shouldn't be used as a point of comparison. I have heard people who have been hurt in life make the statement that no one could ever understand their pain, and for them, that is true. However, the depth of your pain does not take away from my pain. Just as the depth of my pain does not take away from your pain, it is all painful, and it all hurts. We get to practice compassion with our pain and not comparison.

No matter how you were raised, unless you were taught to express your dis-ease in life, you have uncomfortable thoughts and feelings anchored to your past. This connection brings your old lifestyle forward. **When the past occupies the present, it is hard to be mindful of the now.**

As I have learned to recognize my past feelings, I can see that shame dominated my experience within my childhood. Recognizing this shame and being with it has allowed me to find more peace with my youth. As you explore your past lifestyle, what feelings do you notice coming up?

PRISONER OF THE PAST

Your past is a conglomeration of memories you love and fear. The past doesn't have to be something that happened years ago. The past can be something that happened a few moments ago that keeps your mind anchored there rather than being present to what is.

The past is for reflection, not for reliving.

Yet, Dr. Joe Dispenza says that 90% of our thoughts are the same thoughts as the day before. This again is an example of our mind taking up a passive thought process, rather than making an active choice.

You must be willing to remember the past for it to exist in current reality consciously.

As you look backward in life, there will be memories you might desire to relive or redo.

To look back and desire a different outcome than what has happened is an invisible prison of Modern Fear. You are living trapped in a desire that if the past were different, you would be different, which is true. **If your past were different, you would also be different; however, you cannot change the past. You can only change the present moment.** I can't change the fact that I was abused. I can, however, find the acceptance that due to the abuse, I have learned to be resilient, and that is a valuable gift.

"Bad" things happen, which make you feel hurt, sad, and angry. You have a choice on how you react or respond to these experiences.

For every one negative, there are two positives. Seek out the lessons to find positivity in life.

I was in high school when this idea was first introduced to me. When the above words were spoken, my past came rushing toward me like a freight train out of control. I relived the abuse, neglect, abandonment, pain, and suffering. I didn't want to believe that my past had any positivity to it. I endured memory after memory, seeking a positive outcome from what others would consider a tragedy. I wanted to believe that pain was my true story. I justified my rebellious behaviors through the lens of painful experiences.

My anger flared, reliving these moments. Then my fear, my shame, and my self-doubt grew. I struggled to find one positive, let alone two positives.

I was in orchestra class at the time, with my head hung low. My attention was drawn to the violin in my lap. I quietly plucked a string. That is when reality hit me. One of the men who molested me had brought me this violin in the fifth grade. The violin had traveled with me to each of the four middle schools and high school. No matter what city or state I lived in, the violin always brought me, instant friends.

With effort, I was able to find my two positives; creative expression and friends. I was able to shift my perspective from abuse to exploring possibilities of sharing musical joy with others.

Two positives for every negative.

For the first time in my life, I was able to look backward and **accept my past's unchangeable events.** I was able to view them with compassion and acceptance, although at the time, I hadn't learned what compassion and acceptance were. The chaos and turmoil of my mind became calmer. My body relaxed as a wave of relief washed over me as I felt the holds of my past experiences loosen their grips on my current reality.

Establishing a practice of looking for the two positives gave my mind something to focus on rather than suffering in my pain. It opened the possibility of acceptance and gave me a new lens of perspective from which to share my past traumas. I now could share from a place of opportunity to support growth rather than from a space of shame. The practice of looking for two positives for every one negative, saved my life. It changed my thinking trajectory, giving rise to feelings that were once trapped behind these "negative" experiences.

There are always going to be memories you cannot change. You cannot rewrite history. The people, the places, and the events - they are still going to be there.

You have a choice to use your memories to inspire purpose in your life or to hold yourself, prisoner, in the suffering of your mind. It takes practice to master the choice of seeking gifts from experience rather than reliving the actual trespass of abuse. Our internal growth happens after escaping the abuse, and yet our minds can keep us trapped in the moment of harm.

Your past is meant to serve one purpose, and one beneficial purpose only, which is to find acceptance today for the future's greater intentions.

RELIVING THE OLD STORY

We all have stories and memories from our past that lay the foundation for the present, and sometimes they can hold us prisoner to what once was.

I know that for some of us, the past is our glory days. We romance and remember all the great things that once were, wishing to be transported back to a time that felt more exciting. For others, the past is a place of hell that holds us in the suffering of what once was. We can hold onto our past identities so firmly that we cannot identify with what is happening in our life now. When this disconnection to the present occurs, it is challenging to be aware of our impact on ourselves and others.

To re-experience any memory too often will energetically take away from the person you are today. Good or bad, you are chasing feelings you experienced in your past that no longer exist except in you.

Reliving the memory of my abuse kept me within the abuse cycle, giving me an excuse not to respect myself. I was unconsciously seeking the abuse over and over again by making and allowing "bad" choices. In a way, I used my experiences of being victimized as a badge of honor, justifying why I was allowed to hate myself.

I frequently thought about being a victim. I hated being trapped in fear of a person that was no longer there. It made me feel angry. Rage against the trespasses fueled me not to trust anyone. I didn't want to be a victim, as that identity made me feel weak, undeserving, and discarded by the world. Looking back now, I understand that being abused was only the beginning of the damage and pain that I would endure. I would relive the moment of the abuse for a split second, and then I would find myself lost in a spiral of self-disgust and self-abuse. This was my way of trying to control my feelings around the abuse because I could not control the abuser or their actions. I created a sense of false control by seeing myself as responsible for my abuse. This false responsibility amplified the anger I felt towards the experiences, trapping myself further and avoiding my feelings. I questioned, "Why didn't I fight harder," and "why didn't I avoid the situation? Why, why, why?" This attempt to release me from the old story kept me in a different pattern of reliving the abuse.

Our brains will try to rationalize any experience to make sense of it. The brain is responsible for making us safe. When something outside of your control happens, the brain will take over to create an explanation, even if that means giving you a story that is not entirely true. For example, I shared previously about my father and the story my mind created around being abandoned. In his reality, he was doing the best he could with what he had, and there was no malicious intention behind his lack of participation in my life.

I didn't trust anyone while I was carrying around victim energy, which resulted from reliving my abuse stories. This energy manifested as feeling shame around my past, hiding my vulnerable feelings, having regular pity parties, reacting in anger, and always feeling like I had to control everything. I used to stonewall people so they couldn't get too close. I wanted them to know how strong I was. I didn't want people to ever think of me as a victim.

There came a time that I decided I no longer wanted to live as my abused self. I tried to heal from these experiences. The first part of healing was recognizing that I needed to stop reliving the past and allow my present feelings to just be without any judgments.

The hardest part of this healing process was letting myself grieve the experiences of being a victim. My initial response to my abuse was anger. I was angry at feeling the physical experience. Angry at myself for not stopping these things from happening to me. Angry at the people that violated my body. Angry at my mom for failing to protect her children. I was so angry that I couldn't get close to grief; anger was my first defense mechanism, blaming the world and myself.

Then I started to notice little girls that were my age when I went through these traumatic experiences. It broke my heart to think that someone else was willing to violate such an innocent being. I imagined my young self as that little girl, and the overwhelming disgust for the predators

LEAH LOVELIGHT MICHAEL | 43

shifted to heart-wrenching sorrow. I couldn't go back and protect myself. We already know we can't redo the past because the damage has been done. What I was able to do was comfort myself rather than reliving the abuse. Within my imagination, I reassured my young self that we would end up safe. I comforted my inner little girl and let her know that I was there for her, and we wept and held each other.

To break free of reliving being a victim, I surrendered to an intimate relationship with my vulnerability, and I mourned. I couldn't find forgiveness until I found sadness. I had to stop relying on the brute strength that was fueled by my anger. I felt the pain, the abandonment, the isolation, and the sadness. During the mourning process, I finally started to feel comforted by the person I am today.

In my personal experience, I have found a direct correlation between the depths that I am willing to hold myself and honor my grief and the amount of joy I can feel in my present reality. The deeper we dig into ourselves, the higher our energy can soar. It always makes me think of the ancient saying, "As above, so below."

If you are reliving your past and are not proactively manifesting your power in your present life, you are holding yourself, prisoner, within Modern Fear.

THE ABUSE CYCLE - TRAUMA & DRAMA

Our abuse cycle begins with trauma. In my experience, trauma can be an emotional or physical wounding or a disturbing incident that creates an emotional response of dis-ease or distress. Trauma can be done to you or can be something that you have witnessed be done to others.

Trauma creates chaos in our energetic field, forming energy blocks that imprison horrific moments in our physical cells and destroy our ability to trust. We become energetically bonded to these traumas, often subconsciously, which lowers the vibration of our thoughts, feelings, and emotions.

With the release of Modern Fear, I have found that it's not the details of the trauma that is important; it is the willingness to be able to recognize and accept that you have been traumatized. As you practice witnessing the traumatic response within yourself, acknowledge the fear by pausing to notice any energetic constrictions. Pausing allows for an opportunity to contemplate whether the fear or resistance is emotionally, mentally, or physically present, rather than getting swept up in the reaction.

There is a broad spectrum of trauma that can shock our emotional, physical, and mental system; heartbreak, disappointment, and confusion can all be traumatic. Examples of traumatic experiences can be accidents, cancer, death, and the initial experience of abuse.

Trauma typically occurs suddenly, whereas abuse is an experience that we can perpetually live within, either because of a third party or the abuse we do to ourselves.

Abuse can be the result of someone else's actions or words, the environment in which we live, and the lifestyle we choose. Abuse can also be the result of our own thoughts, feelings, and actions towards ourselves. Once we have been traumatized or abused, it is not just the abuser to whom we become a victim, but also the experience itself and thoughts or actions in reaction to the trauma.

When abusers abuse their victims, dark energy is transferred. It is forced upon us or used against us. Our energetic field experiences an attack, and our energy will contract to protect our internal life force. We will hold bits of this dark energy within these constrictions, which act like a virus, infecting our mental, emotional, physical, and energetic fields. This dark energy virus can make us sick with dis-ease, wrapping our energy in an invisible blanket of anger and fear. It is a dangerous time for those experiencing this infection because reactions out of anger are perpetual and can cause destruction and chaos.

At a young age, my brother went through his trauma of abuse by a human lost in dark energy, out of alignment with the greater good. This abuser destroyed my brother on many levels and sent him down the self-destruction path for many years. My brother being abused caused my brother to abuse me, transferring the abuse cycle, which continues to ripple through our energetic connections.

This is, by far, the most challenging part of my story to share. I ask for guidance from Source to hold the lessons that will support the greater good for you as the reader.

My older brother is the source of my most significant trauma, mostly because it is incredibly confusing to be abused by someone that you love. Out of rebellion against his own life experiences, he became a juvenile delinquent and spent many years in and out of juvenile jail and turned to substance abuse. I always felt sorry for my brother. I felt like he was given the short end of the stick, and I was able to feel for him and his experiences empathically. I had completely blocked the full trauma done to me by my brother out of my consciousness, until one day I remembered.

I had spent many years working on healing the memories of my abuse, and I was finally to a place where I felt like I genuinely had an acceptance for what had happened to me. o much so, I got a little cocky and asked if anything else needed to be healed. When the flash of my brother appeared into my consciousness, my body fully recoiled from the shock, and I dropped to the ground sobbing out loud. I declared and prayed, "I don't want to remember this."

This is not the way the universe works. Once you know or remember, you will never be able not to know.

After this memory resurfaced, my brother cycled back into my world by literally moving into my Rock Creek home for a few months. We were driving past the land that my dad once lived on, and I asked my brother, "Do you have any memories from when you were a kid living here?" At the time, he didn't give much of an answer. Later, however, the truth of our childhood came forward.

Sitting at the dining room table, my brother said, "Do you remember when you asked me if I remember being a kid?"

In my gut, I knew what was coming. I could feel the resistance of not wanting to hear what he was going to say. The feeling of shame was bubbling up inside of me. I was terrified of receiving a confirmation of the truth that I knew could hurt our relationship. I wanted to close down and run away from what was going to happen next.

He shared with me the experience of his abuse and then his fear that he had transferred dark energy to me. As I looked at him, my heart was saddened by his experience. I didn't want to cause more harm because I do not believe that my brother's abuse was malevolent. I quickly said to him, "I know, I recently had a memory surface, and you are only confirming what I already remembered." I gave him quick forgiveness because he was a child and didn't fully understand what he was doing. However, I didn't allow myself to grieve the trespasses that he had caused my younger self. I did not honor my feelings. I regressed further into my Modern Fear."

In that moment of confession, my brother did find relief. I, on the other hand, found shame, disgust, repulsion, and violation. I also received some clarity and recognized that my brother had been taking advantage of me my entire life. I became angry at the lifetime of manipulation that came with having a relationship with him. I wish I could say that my feelings are resolved, and yet that would not be true. I am still emotionally dedicated to the processing of this truth, and I recognized that it is vital for me to feel all of my feelings without judgment.

It is confusing when someone who we believe loves us harms us. In the feeling of love, we find the value of trust, and within the trust, we find safety. The action of the abuse breaks trust, so we no longer feel safe;

however, what it does not break is our ability to love. I have been abused by many people who have claimed to love me. As a result, my understanding of love meant that there is a cost associated with being loved. I never considered the value of my safety. Instead, I accepted that the price I was willing to pay for being loved was the abuse I received from my abusers.

I allowed myself to stay in abusive situations because I didn't believe I deserved any better. I justified staying because the abuser brought security. Lost in fear, I couldn't see a way out and did not have the confidence to provide my own sense of security. Perhaps the most challenging and most triggering truth for me was that I stayed in the abuse because I thought my abusers loved me; at the time, I couldn't comprehend that love is a life-giving force and not a binding requirement.

Looking backward now, I know that out of protection for myself, I took this experience of my abuse and erased it from my consciousness. That's the funny thing about our mind, it likes to play games, and it is so malleable, **but our body never forgets.** Trauma and abuse move into the cells of our body, creating energetic constrictions. When we experience trauma, our body will naturally contract to protect itself, and within that contraction, we form an invisible prison around that feeling. Consciously, we can't identify why this feeling and experience happened, because our mind has us on lockdown.

Abuse can be a vivid experience that is replayed in the mind. It can also be an unidentified subconscious experience. Both will ripple through life and create an energetic pull for these types of experiences to happen again and again.

As with the law of attraction, like attracts like, abuse attracts abuse.

Abuse is a cycle that has an energetic force that will exist in perpetuity. The choice of one person to harm another, or to self-harm themselves, has residual effects, even if we are not consciously aware of the harm we are doing or are in denial of our current reality.

You might find what I am about to say to be triggering. Often out of frustration, anger, desperation, sadness, and confusion, a victim will become an abuser. I know in my journey through the abuse cycle, the most challenging truth I had to accept was that I, too, had become an abuser.

The abuse that I received from my brother was a direct result of the abuse that he received from an adult. As children, we mimic experience, it is part of our developmental process, and the cycle is planted within us. To google, the abuse rate of children is shocking, as millions of cases, each year are reported. Imagine what the future holds for all of these children as they navigate through life and the abuse cycle. How will they treat themselves, and who are they going to abuse?

When we are traumatized, our brain will make sense of the situation, and we will replicate what is being done to us in one form or another. As children coming from an abusive situation, most of us have no idea what we are doing as we move from being a victim to being an abuser, trying to regain some sort of control in a situation. If we can't control our reactive feelings, we will try to influence and control others.

As victims, we do not consciously set out to become an abuser. I promise if you take a step back and objectively look at your life, you will be able to see the abuse cycle, and you will be able to rewire it. Moving out of the abuse cycle is not only about not being a victim, but it is also about not being an abuser anymore.

Out of protection, I tried to harden myself so that future abusers couldn't get in. In the hardening process, I became bitter, and I started to lash out at the world. As my rage surfaced, I spoke cruel words to make sure I cut others, deeply harming my relationships. I have been the meanest to the people I love the most, and this truth humbles me. I work daily on karmic realignment of this vibration in my energetic field. One of the most triggering truths is the awareness of our mood and its effect on others. When we are within the low energetics of abusive behavior, pity parties, and self-centered absorption, the low mood emanates from us, causing other people within our homes or life to feel uncomfortable around us. When left unchecked, this can become mildly abusive behavior.

Even if you are not abusing others, from my experience of being a victim and witnessing other victims, I have noticed that the primary person we abuse is ourselves. Either through negative self-talk, substance abuse, physical abuse, promiscuity, and this list could go on. These are all signs of self-abuse.

Most of the time, we become the abuser of our own being. We will say awful, hurtful things to ourselves; "What is wrong with me?" "Why am I so stupid?" "I deserve to be treated like this." We allow our bodies to become unattractive by gaining excessive weight or by losing too much and becoming a walking skeleton. We sink out of humanity, attempting to prevent ourselves from being seen, either by getting lost within alternative virtual realities that occupy our waking hours or just being so depressed that getting out of bed becomes impossible.

For the victims out there, here is a key to the universe that will change your life. **The last person you will stop abusing is yourself.** No matter how far you have transmuted your victim experience until you are compassionate, kind, and forgiving of yourself, you will remain trapped as a victim. Even the smallest amount of abuse will hold you, prisoner, in Modern Fear.

If you have been a victim, take a moment right now to recognize where you have been an abuser. It is the only way to stop the cycle. Unless we become brave enough to stop the abusive behavior within our own field of existence, we will continue to repeat this cycle.

When we are abused and victimized, something is being done to us. This violation is a cruel act, and honestly, I feel it is a dangerous trap because when we are victimized, we ascertain: "This was done to me." While true, this statement can plant deep roots in our subconscious and get us caught deeper in the abuse cycle as we take on the victim's identity.

In the last words I spoke to my brother, I claimed the identity of being his victim. I angrily said, "I am so glad you have done work around your abuse; however, I am still your victim." That proclamation gave my energetic power to my abuser. I was saying it to hurt him, and in reality, it deeply hurt us both. I don't want to be a victim to anyone or any circumstance, and yet, the truth of real experience is complicated. There are many layers in the reclaiming and rewiring of the energetics around abuse.

I do have forgiveness for my brother's actions; they were not out of spite. I do have compassion for his own experience and the trauma drama that he will get to heal. Most importantly, I have deep gratitude for being given the opportunity to discover the abuse cycle and the steps to break it.

When we abuse, harm, or belittle others, we are causing someone, even ourselves, to feel like a victim. Physical, mental, verbal, or emotional abuse, no matter how horrific or insignificant the intention, hurts. These actions are wounding.

In this section, I honestly struggled with what to share as I questioned myself on what parts of my story I want to give life. I share this discomfort so that I can express the importance of sharing our personal stories from a place of healing and not from a place of being further lost in the trauma drama of our experiences.

The stories that we create to justify or rationalize an experience that we share to relate to someone else are what I refer to as our drama. The "I was wronged" perspective, which we hold onto so tightly, can become the abuse dramas. We saw so many people put their hands up during the "Me Too" movement uniting around the fact that another harmed us. There was a revolutionary ripple that led to the accusations and prosecution of people who had wronged others. Yet, I feel during the #metoo movement, we missed learning how we each healed from the trespasses, moving through our transformations of trauma.

Drama follows trauma because it is confounding when trauma happens. Our minds, in natural defense, begin to make up a story to explain the reason for this trauma.

In the fifth grade, during one of the "stranger danger" discussions, my teacher Mr. Adcock showed the class a black and white photo and told us that if a person ever touches you in a way that doesn't feel right, we could always tell him.

My heart was racing as I approached the room's front after he had put us to work on an assignment. He looked up at me with the kindest eyes, "Can I help you?" I was terrified, fighting to hold back the tears, "Ummm, you know how you showed us the picture? Well, my neighbor touches me in those ways."

Mr. Adcock's eyes grew so wide. I knew this was not what he was expecting me to say. He recovered quickly and moved into an action plan. He busied the other students and took me into the next room to ask me for more details. The school called my mom, and when she was told what happened, she looked right at me and said, "Are you sure?"

I will never forget that question. "Are you sure?"

From that moment and to this day, that question still dances around my thoughts as a betrayal of protection. I was a scared little girl, and more than anything, I wanted my mom to hold me and keep me safe, but she couldn't. In her shock of the situation, she responded in disbelief, which made me feel like I had done something wrong and not our neighbor.

The night before I shared the situation with Mr. Adcock, our neighbor, Ted, had taken our family out to dinner at a local German restaurant in Missoula. He often treated us, and it was always the best because of the all-you-could-eat salad bar. Every time we ate there, I would gorge myself, all of that food, and I could have anything I wanted. Ted spoiled us often "financially." The price was the innocence of children. That night when Ted dropped us off, I ran inside and looked out the window at my older sister, who was still in the car with him. I witnessed an embrace that made me sick, I knew it wasn't right, and I wondered what I could do about it. During class the next day, I received a sign from the universe, and I told my teacher about Ted, except I said that Ted was touching me, which at the time I didn't actually believe. Because of the other abuse I had already experienced, I had become good at disassociating from my emotions and body as a form of subconscious protection. I had no memory of being touched. I only had the image of the embrace with my sister in my thoughts.

At the police station, the officers were gentle with me. I was sitting at a table, and sheets of paper were placed in front of me, with pictures of little girl figures on them. "Please draw a circle around the places that he touched you." At that moment, I was terrified. What was I doing? I sat there in pure panic and shock, and then picked up the pencil and started circling parts on the girl figures. What if I couldn't remember what I circled? What if I got in trouble for what I was doing? I had none of these memories. I only wanted to protect my big sister.

As the trial approached, I made myself sick with worry. I was in over my head, and I knew it. I was just a ten-year-old kid.

Then we received word that Ted had pleaded guilty, and there would be no trial.

Secretly, I was so confused. Why did he plead guilty? I couldn't make sense of Ted's confession, even though I was deeply relieved there would be no trial. Ted was sentenced by the courts and was sent to a mental institution due to being found mentally ill.

I was twenty-seven years old before I remembered what had happened with Ted. I had repressed my memories, and when they surfaced, I felt like a freight train hit me. It was a typical day, and I was in the shower washing my hair, eyes closed, and out of nowhere, my thoughts flashed to an image of his bedroom and then quickly to his kitchen table as he pulled me to him. I could smell his cologne and could hear Patsy Cline playing in the background.

I crumbled in the shower, shaking violently, the water running until it went cold.

The complexity of this story is that I had been repressing my own experiences. For most of my life, I thought I had made up being molested by Ted and that my fifth-grade self had projected a story that I was protecting my sister. I had created a drama around my experience because I couldn't endure the feelings of my heartbreaking truths.

To use our voice and to be able to share our trauma is vital for healing. It is crucial to allow for the anger, sadness, and grief to surface so that it can pass; however, if we continue to share our trauma seeking comradery, we are reinforcing that traumatic experience and destroying our ability to transcend the experience through healing.

The details of the wound are not what is important. Yes, they could create an opportunity for you and me to relate around our trauma drama; however, this would keep us in Modern Fear because the pain of the wounds blocks out the ability to feel anything else.

I don't want you to relate to me as a victim. I want you to be inspired by my liberty from this prison.

What dramas are you living in right now? The way we speak about our abuse and what was done to us is fundamental to break the abuse cycle; we can stay a victim within our drama and the abuse story that we share unless it is spoken from a space of forgiveness.

I say all of this because I discovered layers upon layers, drama, and stories stacked on more drama and stories in my own healing journey. My mind has had an excellent capacity for keeping me safe, and it only let me remember what I could handle at any given time. Every time I have thought, I am finally "healed," I have discovered more. This is why a healing journey is called "work." There isn't an easy button on this journey. However, every layer I have taken off has enabled me to breathe deeper, which allows me to continue to move forward.

If you choose to tell your story from a perspective of healing, then the power of the painful memories will begin to shift into a deep well of inspiration that can be used to support and guide others who might still be lost in their own suffering.

THE DRAIN OF TOXIC PEOPLE

We all have a toxic person in our life, at home, at work, or within a group of friends.

Toxic people are depleting. They belittle others and are blind to their behaviors, often feeling like they are the ones that are misunderstood. They believe they are in the right and will make sure you know it.

They are bullies and make sure to push the blame onto others for their abusive tendencies. This is how they cop-out from taking responsibility for their behaviors. They are instigators. They feed their energy by taking away yours.

As low-level abusers, toxic people are out for their self-absorbed gain. They neglect to pay attention to others' feelings. As a result of being around them, you are training yourself to ignore your feelings. This is a skilled pattern that we practice throughout our lives.

When you allow someone into your life who does not treat you with respect, they will become a conflict point. **Their behaviors and treatment toward you will confuse your perception of how you think other people see you.**

For example, I am a woman who speaks up. I am not afraid to say it like it is. For many years people perceived me as a bitch. I played into this identity as it was true on a survival level because of how I grew up. Until one day, it wasn't, and I consciously tried to be a kinder person.

I was at my friend's bar, and I said something direct to the bartender, and my friend said, "Leah, you are such a bitch."

And I looked him directly in the eyes and said, "No, I am not." My friend was trying to build himself up by talking down to me and devaluing my character. This toxic behavior was being justified due to my past actions. Not for the person I was at that moment. Toxic people will continue to remind and punish you from missteps from your past.

Allowing toxic patterned behaviors constructs cells within the invisible prison of Modern Fear and will cause your reactive anxiety to increase. The pain and dis-ease that toxic people cause will spread into your world, and you will become reactive because this is part of the abuse cycle, even at low levels. Be it through a small outburst misdirected at someone you care about or the exhaustion from the toxicities upon your body, mind, and soul.

Our society fosters a culture that allows toxic people to thrive because they are dramatic, and as humans, we love to be entertained. Love him or hate him; Donald Trump is an excellent example of a person who uses toxic behaviors for demoralizing and entertaining the masses. He causes intentional chaos and doesn't care about the consequences due to his narcissism. For the most part, toxic people in the general public are often a nuisance and lack consideration for others. For example, I heard a story of someone yelling at a Costco cashier because they were out of toilet paper, and no one did anything to stop this person from verbally assaulting another human. This is an example of how toxic people can impose the effects of the ripple of fear on others.

The toxicity becomes a personal problem when toxic people are found in your workplace, home, or immediate group of friends because these are places that you cannot avoid. This is why it is crucial to recognize who is in your life. Call a spade a spade, and create the space you need, not allowing these toxic people to impact you.

Toxic people can be too clever at hiding their characters. They can put forth a false identity, which makes them appear a certain way, and they can become part of your life before you fully recognize them for what they are.

Toxic people's behavior will cause you pain and suffering if you allow them to remain. You could become toxic yourself if you are not consciously aware of the conversations you are having in your head or are not taking responsibility for how you are living your life.

Toxic people are not always aware of their behaviors, as we can become toxic out of a reaction to difficulties within our own lives. As we move through recognizing the toxic effects in our lives and identifying the source of toxicity, there is an opportunity to potentially support another human that is going through their own pain.

I challenge you to ask yourself why? Why invest your time and energy into a person who will suck it out of you willingly? Be kind to yourself in this process, because this is a practice of becoming conscious of how others impact your energy.

As we grow older, each of us develops differently. A best friend from the past could become a stranger to the present. Value and beliefs evolve, and they don't always evolve simultaneously for each person in a relationship. When we recognize that someone we once loved and enjoyed no longer brings the same inspiration into our lives, it doesn't mean we no longer care about them. It just means they no longer align with us.

I have heard myself and others say that love and loyalty to a once significant past is another reason we stay in toxic relationships. The past is gone. It only exists in your thoughts. The present, right now, is the only time that matters. The excuse of love can be toxic and detrimental to your well-being because the loyalty we have to this love holds us imprisoned within Modern Fear. We are not allowing ourselves to truly feel the toxicity's pain as we hide behind the notion of love.

You do play a part in this relationship. You allow these people to be part of your life, giving excuse after excuse because you remember who they were before they "became" toxic. This is not intended to create shame, because we are all duped by toxic people in one way or another. The real reflection here is: if you have toxic people in your life, and you know that they are toxic, why are they still in your life?

There are only a few choices when dealing with toxic people and the breaking free of the imprisonment you have allowed to be created inside of you. This acknowledgment is a difficult step because none of us want to be responsible for allowing our mental, emotional, and spiritual beings to be impacted negatively.

The first choice to deal with toxic people seems the easiest. Cut them out of your life. Forget that they exist. Except that cutting someone out of our life isn't that easy or practical. If we are cutting this person out of our life as a reactionary response to their toxic choices, we can experience residual pain in response to the grief that comes from our cruel behavior. There is no proper closure with this choice. However, this example does not negate that sometimes cutting someone out is the best response to preserve your peace of mind and heal from their impact on your life. This choice can be incredibly difficult when it comes to family or friends.

The other option is trying to bring light to the behavior while allowing the toxic person to reform. You want the person to remain in your life without the toxicity, but the stress and anxiety they create make it hard for you to express your feelings due to their emotional manipulation. Give yourself space so that you may ask yourself what you need within this relationship to survive the toxicity. Explore what boundaries need to be established so that you may have sovereignty over your feelings in this toxic person's presence.

A powerful tool to shift a relationship with a toxic person is empathy.

For a moment, step back from your experience with this person, and get into their shoes. We are all either reacting or responding to a feeling within ourselves. This simple yet profound practice can change your perspective and allow you to empathize with what might be causing others' behaviors. If you get curious about why they behave in such a toxic way, it will enable your perspective to shift. Rather than thinking about the dis-ease they are causing you, you can think about their cause. The power of empathy can be a powerful way to defuse your reaction and disrupt this low-level abuse cycle.

This empathetic perspective does not justify the awful behavior, not for a minute. This shift in perspective sets an energetic boundary; witnessing the toxic person's heartache allows you the opportunity to be around this person without the toxic invasion because you have an understanding that this is their pain, not yours.

You are not meant to carry the suffering of others. Your own life will bring this lesson forward. Invest your energy into those who invest theirs back into you.

Be willing to clearly and specifically identify the feelings you allow others to influence if you want to heal this state of disease in your life.

Just as you have a choice of letting that toxic person remain in your life, that toxic person has a choice regarding their behaviors.

In the practice of contemplation, you can become fascinated with why you feel uncomfortable or anxious about the relationship with the toxic person.

The effects of toxicity have a breaking point, as it is not sustainable energy. There will come a time when you must look inside yourself, be honest, and seek the truth that is imprisoned inside of you. You are worthy of meaningful relationships that support your growth.

Your feelings matter. You do not deserve to be treated with disrespect, abuse, or neglect.

Give your toxic person a chance for reform but do not allow them to continue their behavior around you. **Stand up for yourself.**

Recognizing that the abuse cycles, trauma, dramas, old stories, and toxic people are in our lives to present opportunities for us to grow through uncomfortable situations boldly, and help us build perseverance and resilience. Open the door to this invisible prison, release yourself from this Modern Fear that prevents you from being the co-creator of your reality.

ANTICIPATORY ANXIETY

"Our anxiety does not empty tomorrow of its sorrows,
but only empties today of its strengths."
Charles Haddon Spurgeon

Anxiety is a symptom of fear. It is part of the freeze chemical response of the brain, and in small doses, is a useful tool for facilitating mental preparation for situations that feel uncomfortable. For example, prepping for taxes always makes me feel a little anxious, and I avoid doing it until the deadline forces me to take action with an intense feeling of anxiety due to having put it off for so long. This is a vicious cycle, and I know I am not alone.

The anxious mind is not always a bad thing. A nervous feeling can indicate that your mind has deemed an upcoming event as significant and wants you to pay close attention to the details. This feeling fosters internal dialogues and acceleration when a call to action is necessary, pushing you into strategy mode. Learning to feel and allowing anxious feelings to put you into motion could support your relationship with anxiety.

Anxiety holds us in a loop of intrusive thoughts that become reactive to an anticipatory response to fear. An obsessive internal dialogue that has taken root without conscious permission impacts our mind, body, and psyche. As we become trapped in Modern Fear, our feelings are shut down except for what is reacting to the stimulus of discomfort.

Your mind becomes fixated on what I call hamster wheel questions, for example:
- What if?
- Why does this always happen to me?
- Should I?

The buildup of this repetitive fixation can become so intense that it does more harm than good, crushing the ability to act. This often results

60 | MODERN FEAR: THE INVISIBLE PRISON

in mental isolation, hyper-focused thoughts, pushing others away, and blaming external stimuli as the source of dis-ease. It is usually an external stimulus that might trigger our anxiety. The idea of being around a bunch of people is stressful to me; however, my anxiety no longer gets the best of me because of the internal conversations I have in preparation for going out into public.

I learned about the prison of "What if" while I was on a layover in Laos.

When I boarded the small, packed plane, I saw a man already in his aisle seat. I noticed him noticing me and felt a calming presence about him as I moved past on the way to my seat.

When we landed for the layover, I planned to get caught up on my travel blog. I sat down on the terminal floor and plugged in my laptop. When the guy walked up to me and asked if I wanted to get coffee at the place across the way, I jumped up with a strong yes. After traveling for a while, I had learned it is these types of connections that matter and often bring learning.

We sat and talked as he sipped coffee and I snacked on banana pancakes.

I shared with him that I was the type of person that has back-up plans for back-up plans. I never approach a situation without thinking about what I would say if (fill in the blank), or what I would do if (fill in the blank). What I didn't realize was that I was lost in my desire to control outcomes, and I had no idea that I was preventing the opportunity to trust that the universe will provide.

He looked me dead in the eye, and he said, "You are never going to know."

A stranger from a faraway land who taught professional downhill speed skiers to visualize their success changed my life forever. He was a mind coach who gave me the gift of realizing that I am never going to know someone else's response, and I should just share where and how I am feeling in that moment, rather than making myself reactive to and anxious of the outcome. I am eternally thankful for this awareness, as it has allowed me to move from the confines of my head, thinking I could control outcomes, and into the allowance of any exchange in life.

You can run every single "what if" scenario in your head that you want.

The truth is, you DON'T KNOW. The future is undetermined, and people are going to have their own experiences.

Remember to make room for other people's feelings when you are planning on having an uncomfortable conversation. Pre-planning "what if's" are not giving them a chance to participate in the potential agreed-upon outcome. By doing this, you are taking their power away while trying to manipulate the scenario for your best possible results. Your extensive overthinking has the potential to hit that person with a ton of bricks. You are trying to win a war when the other party might not even know a battle exists.

In my own "what if" prison, I was so afraid of messing up and hurting someone's feelings that I tried to control everything, which was exhausting. For example, I cannot even count the number of times I had a conversation with myself before asking my ex-husband for a divorce. I was so mean to myself, highlighting all my flaws for things not working rather than sharing responsibility for the situation. This stranger, a man that crossed my path in Laos, was telling me that I was never going to know how someone else would respond. By me not sharing my feelings or thoughts with others, I was taking away their opportunity to engage in the experience.

For me to rewire my "what if" prison, I had to consciously stop myself from getting on the "what if" hamster wheel. I would actively say, "no, what if," and replace that phrase with "what is in front of me now?"

To know the root of your anticipatory anxiety is a powerful tool; it is the door to freedom from the control it has over you. **Fear is meant to be a survival response, not a constant life passenger.**

To discover the root, we practice witnessing the mental, emotional, and physical bodies and the symptoms being expressed.

- Obsessive thinking about what is not working.
- Motivational paralysis.
- A physical sensation of claustrophobia with an increased heart rate and restricted breathing.
- A complete meltdown.

These are just a few symptoms that can be experienced, not to be confused as the cause or the trigger.

62 | MODERN FEAR: THE INVISIBLE PRISON

Modern Fear that causes stress and anxiety makes you more prone to illness, weight gain, crappy sleep, and poor decision making.

Get curious with yourself and ask yourself these example questions:

- How often does your stomach hurt when you are stressed out?
- How often when you are stressed out do you get a headache?
- How often do you lie awake at night thinking about the same thing over and over again, getting further and further away from falling asleep?
- How easy is it after a stressful day to swing through a fast-food restaurant making poor nutrition choices?

I invite you to take five minutes here and explore some of the ways you experience anxiety. Notice your body, your emotions, and your thoughts. Write down the signs and symptoms or sensations you are experiencing, allow for them to be present, get curious.

There is a way out of Modern Fear rooted in your anxiety.

You will need to use your detective skills and do some deep inner self-work. Most importantly, be a good listener of your inner wisdom, accept the truth, and take responsibility.

Ask yourself, "Why do I have anticipatory anxiety?" Listen to your body, heart, and mind. Feel the truth as it ripples through your awareness, like an "Ah-ha" that can't be ignored. As thoughts and feelings arise within you, pause with these moments, and experience them for precisely what they are rather than judging the situation.

You will get many answers; however, do not be satiated by the answers that come quickly. These are on the surface and will only bring temporary relief. Easy solutions are like the cell windows of your prison; they are an illusion of freedom. You'll know when a more resonant answer surfaces because it will capture your full attention. You will often experience this awareness in your mind, body, and feelings. When an easy answer, surfaces, ask, "Is there more?" Pause and see what reveals itself. This contemplative approach allows internal permission to release more profoundly into the inquisition of truth.

Only when you discover the deeper root of the truth will you find the finish line of your anticipatory anxiety in Modern Fear.

WHEN ANXIOUS TURNS TO REACTIVE

The ultimate consequence of unchecked anxiety is being primed to blow our fuse. We live in a high-stress world; an increased workload, pressure for societal "success," and emotional suppression all cause anxiety.

In stressful environments that cannot be avoided, we tend to emotionally censor our vulnerability, locking away and suppressing our true feelings. Repeated exposure to the same unavoidable, stressful environment, like school, work, and even your own home, becomes a trigger for reactive anxiety. Mentally, though perhaps not consciously, you identify the environment as damaging and automatically set up emotional defenses. Not having an opportunity to release the stress of suppressed feelings and building an internal defense creates a build-up of energy within ourselves that can become reactive if triggered by an unexpected situation. These situations create a compounding effect and ultimately lead to more reactions. Unless there is a safe and healthy opportunity to release these feelings, anxiety will continue to build.

The compounding effects of dread or procrastination lead to increased anxiety, which, in turn, leads to more dread and procrastination. Before you know it, you are in a reactive and explosive state of anxiety. For example, you have a co-worker who you don't get along with, and you are assigned a project together. Instantly, you begin to think about all the reasons why this won't work, yet it is your job, so you know you are required to complete this project even though the idea is making you sick. Eventually, after procrastinating, the time comes, and you start the project; however, within just a few minutes of working together, something blows your fuse, and you storm out of the task declaring that you can never work with this person again.

In a reactive state of anxiety, you have lost control over your feelings about your situation. You are off your rocker, and nothing can be said to bring you back because reasoning is not available to you. Reactive anxiety has now impacted your ability to perform what is required of you.

Due to reactive anxiety, your body has entered into a permanent state of fight or flight mode, and you are causing yourself harm due to the release of stress hormones, which could eventually lead to adrenal fatigue or worse.

Your focus decreases, causing you to forget important details, often unrelated to the situation, like when your partner asks you to bring home some milk. At the end of a stressful day, you completely forget about this promise. This leads to more reactive anxiety when you get home as your partner is upset with you for ignoring their needs.

Your performance falters, which leads to a breakdown of trust in you by others because you become unreliable. You seek escape and look for ways to numb or avoid, which breaks down your internal trust of self.

Reactive anxiety amplifies Modern Fear by blinding you to a rational perspective. You know something is wrong. You can feel it throughout your body; the tension headache, the upset stomach, and the increased fatigue all keep you in a constant state of dis-ease.

While trying to justify or explain the dis-ease, you are in, cue the blame game.

The "if only" excuse controls your self-talk, and your attention is focused outward because inward feels overwhelmed.

- "If only your spouse would pitch in some more."
- "If only your boss understood the workload."
- "If only others understood what you are going through."

There is no good in the statement of "if only." These two words trap you in powerlessness because you are wanting the external world to alter your internal reality, thus leading to more reactive anxiety.

Just like when you open up a carbonated beverage that has been tossed around a few times, it is essential to let out a little bit of the pressure at times to avoid being in an explosive mess. A great way to release built-up tension is to practice deep intentional breathing, with an audible sigh on the exhale.

PROCRASTINATION

The dread of responsibility or fear of an outcome gives us reasons to avoid something that we know we have to do.

Procrastination is avoidance in action.

We can procrastinate in so many ways; physically, we can choose not to take the necessary action. We can verbally hold back our voice to avoid a more complicated conversation, and mentally our thoughts can pretty much talk us out of anything. It isn't too hard to justify our choices.

Holding back our thoughts, actions, and voice to avoid potential confrontation or responsibility is procrastinating, and this practice directs our energy into an invisible prison because we feel undervalued, unseen, unheard, and unappreciated.

Instead of actively doing what should be done, our mind creates inner stories that distract our intentions and ultimately leads us to a state of Modern Fear out of shame and disappointment in ourselves.

Procrastinating often means there is a one-sided conversation happening inside of your head, creating stories about the "why" or possible outcomes. Procrastination due to poor communication or potential confrontation will hurt any relationship. In unavoidable environments, for example, a conflict with your partner, if you do not stand up for yourself by procrastinating necessary communication, energetically, you are telling yourself that you are not important.

Due to reactive anxiety and the worry of what might happen, you lose control over yourself, giving your power away. All of your choices have an immediate global effect on your life. When you choose to hold back energetically, then you suffer the consequences, experiencing a sense of scarcity because our external world mirrors our internal state of being.

Your emotional, mental, and physical bodies are all affected by procrastination. Mentally, stacking responsibility upon responsibility creates a toxic overwhelm. We develop a habit of avoidance, where instead of physically doing the necessary task, we might mindlessly scroll on social media instead. Procrastination is emotionally breaking trust with ourselves. Energetically, when you agree, even if you are the only one that hears that agreement and you don't follow through, you are breaking your trust.

Are you procrastinating your greater good? We are all born with a unique purpose. You might not know what it is right now, yet there is an inner knowing, a fire deep inside of you that is waiting to be released. Fear of your potential fire may be holding you in procrastination.

I have known for years that writing this book is a necessary step to support my greater good. Yet, over the last four years, I have allowed many excuses for the procrastination of writing. Fear of my own fire and excuse-making became habituated patterns that required an interrupt to change.

If you practice procrastination and are living inside the invisible prison of Modern Fear away from your feelings, then your quality of life will reflect one that is living out of habit, rather than choice.

The best tool to support the rewiring of procrastination is to check in with my future self before making any decisions in the now.

A classic example of procrastination for me involves the dishes. I love waking up in the morning to a clean kitchen. I mean, it brings me such joy, and just it starts the day off right. However, I also love not having to do the dishes and enjoy my evening.

Before I found the practice of asking my future self, the typical scenario would be me avoiding the dishes in the evening. I would wake up in the morning to a messy kitchen, and almost every single time, I would shame myself for being lazy the night before. This was a brutal cycle, a dirty kitchen, and being mean to myself was not a good start to the day.

Then I discovered I could create a choice. In the evening, when I have a bunch of dishes to wash, and I just don't want to, I imagine myself walking into the kitchen in the morning and asking my future self, "Do you mind doing the dishes for me in the morning?"

Sometimes the answer is "no," and I will leave the dishes. Sometimes the answer is "yes," and then I get to ask my present self, "Can you please do the dishes tonight so we can support our future self?" Sometimes the answer is "yes," and I do the dishes.

However, sometimes the answer is "no." Now I have a future self and a present self; neither wants to do the dishes and obviously, someone has to step forward. At this point, if I decide I don't want to do the dishes that evening, I promise myself no future shame, and if I do the dishes, I make sure in the morning when I walk into that kitchen to give my past self so much gratitude for stepping up.

I invite you to practice asking your future-self permission to evaluate if procrastination is truly necessary. "Do it now, or do it later?"

THE FOUR LETTER WORD – H*TE

It feels gross writing this section, and yet it might be one of the most critical recognitions humanity is destined to face. I create an intentional boundary because I feel my energy constricts to protect myself from h*te's frequency.

On many levels, humanity is lost in the defense mechanism of h*te, which is why we have toxicity, because somewhere deep down inside, we don't like something about ourselves.

I am fully aware of the destructive, powerful energy of h*te. It is like a junkyard dog that I would never let out of my sight. H*te is not going anywhere any time soon. We all need to accept that h*te is a real feeling that many people experience and is something that we will face. Set a boundary around it, so you don't get too close. Even in writing this section, I refuse to give the word any additional power by inserting an * within it to break up the pattern of the word.

H*te is an immensely toxic fire that devours the soul; it is an infectious, energetic virus that invades our physical and emotional beings. Anger, judgment, and resentment are the fuel that keeps the fire burning. For example, racism that grew from systemic h*te. Fear, insecurity, and scarcity pitted the American people against each other. People began to believe that there is no harm in spitting painful words or actions at others, especially if they feel justified.

H*te has detrimental effects on our ability to love. Being caught in the sticky trap of h*te exiles you from the tender nurture of love.

It is easy to think about h*te being something that is outside of you and not something that is inside of you. Yet, when you speak toxically, you give h*ate life. When you feel it, you give it life. We, as humans, are responsible for the perpetuation of h*te.

I have had many run-ins with h*te. I have h*ted people that have harmed me, and I have h*ted myself for the harm that I have caused. What has been done to me, what I have done to myself and others, gave me reasons to h*te. I couldn't see beyond my suffering, which made me lose the value of life, sucking me deeper into the entrapment of my own personal h*te. I was reactive with so much anger that my actions felt vindicated, and I was wrong.

Two wrongs do not make a right. Rather than continuing the perpetuation of my painful story, I worked through one tender memory after another, seeking an opportunity to forgive. This practice allowed me to reclaim my taken energy. Through forgiveness, these stories could be put to rest.

Don't get me wrong, I still get angry, and I still feel rage, except now it is supported by love, leading to effective communication rather than driven by h*te, which causes chaos, anger, and eventually more h*te. Be brave and take inventory of where h*te is present within yourself so that you can rewire this frequency with regenerative forgiveness through love.

THE MENTAL CELL OF DOUBT

Doubt is a component of self-fear that causes your mind to worry. There is nothing like the overwhelming, heavy, slow fear when you doubt your capability. The insecurity is crippling and prevents trusting yourself, holding you within Modern Fear.

Doubt steals time, takes away momentum, and holds you where you are, stealing your productive imagination, and crushing potential dreams.

If someone, like your parents, spouse, or a toxic, abusive person, tells you that your dream is silly, stupid, impossible, or even questions your intentions, they are planting a seed of doubt. Other people's unsupportive thoughts about your goals can cause you to doubt yourself, stopping the momentum of your dreams. This can be a painful experience for anyone. It is important to remember that when other people doubt you, it is a projection of their insecurities around their capabilities.

I invite you to reflect on what happens when others doubt your dreams. More importantly, what do you allow yourself to feel in response to their doubt?

Let's use the tool of curiosity and examine what would happen if you were to side with doubt versus having an internal conversation with doubt.

When you side with doubt, you become embarrassed. You believe you dreamed too big. You discredit your idea, devaluing your belief system, leading to a feeling of worthlessness, and ultimately shame. The negative self-talk takes over, and your dream is now an inmate of an invisible prison.

You could side with the doubters and believe that your dream is impossible, or you could acknowledge that their doubt is their fear response to your dreams. Have an internal conversation with your doubts, ask where is the fear coming from, what is the worst that can happen, or what might be the best possible outcome? The questions give you an understanding of your feelings, allowing for self-compassion, which will reinforce your eagerness for your dream. This is a way to flip the perspective of doubt, especially when it is coming from an external source.

Sometimes doubt comes from within. When there is insecurity within your own being, there is an energetic thread that is tied to the fear of worthiness and deservedness. When the doubt emerges from within, what if you paused and questioned the genuine fear behind this doubt? Curiosity can be used as a tool within the fear of doubt to uncover incredible wisdom from within.

SHAME

Every single one of us knows the feeling of shame. I most certainly know the painful feeling of humiliation and loss of self-respect.

Shame can also be attached to not having situations or things to feel shame around. I know plenty of people that feel shame for having safety, security, and stability when others have so little. I struggle with shaming myself for my success because, as I have moved out of lower socioeconomic status, I have been asked, "Who do you think you are?" "Do you think you are better than us?" Another example is how we have recently seen many white people suffering in their shame of not being conscious of the truth of our nation's full history. Some white people are projecting personal shame and guilt upon the black community for their lack of awareness, which is a debilitating cycle that needs to end. The reality is, shaming never helps; it is depletive energy and will send us into a downward spiral.

Most of my shame comes from my earlier years in life when I didn't want to feel, and I was actively numbing myself.

The abuse of self-shaming is one of the worst that I have ever experienced. I know that the cruelest person that I have ever encountered is myself.

Shame is saying, "I am embarrassed for who I am."

I spent many years of my life hiding parts of myself because I was ashamed and embarrassed. My mental practice was cruel and shaming, locking my energy within the invisible prison of Modern Fear. Shame made me feel like life's spirit had deserted me. I didn't care enough to be kind to myself, nor did I give other people a chance to value and appreciate me. My behavior of shame isolated me further and further away from those who loved me.

Shame is like solitary confinement within our invisible prison. It is devastatingly lonely. Being in a desolate state of shame imprisons our attention and prevents us from being able to experience the joy in the world around us.

Dale Carnegie said, "**Fear** doesn't exist anywhere except in the mind." I am going to evolve this saying a little further and say, "**Shame** doesn't exist anywhere except in the mind."

Shame is a confusing feeling. Initially, it appears that an outside influence sources shame. However, as I have tracked my feelings of shame, I have learned that it originates from within me. Why else do we become embarrassed if we trip and no one else is around?

I was ashamed of where I came from, and reckless behaviors in my past, making me afraid of being judged by others. Consequently, I presented myself in the way I thought the world wanted me to be so that I could blend in. I created internalized expectations of myself. Instead of valuing my uniqueness, I began putting on a mask that was not sincere to who I was, lying to myself, hiding from others, which created more shame within this dishonest way of being.

I see this behavior in so many other people with whom I interact, hiding behind an energy block of shame. This is a tragedy that I hope to rewire in humanity. The gift of each of our lives is our uniqueness, which is lived out through our experiences. You are special, you are unique, and only you bring forward your genius to this world.

We can forget to honor uniqueness because of the natural habit of comparing ourselves to others, which can lead to more shame.

Shame is an epidemic of social media and mainstream entertainment. Look at what you are comparing yourself to these days. The practice of comparison destabilizes the identity of self. Instead of trying to amplify your inner genius, you are trying to mold into something that might not be authentic to you, wasting precious energy.

Due to the media and other "news" platforms, society has become desensitized to people being mean, disrespectful, behaving in risqué ways, and shoving self-absorbed ego into the universe. From my perspective, it is the ego that creates comparison, which leads us to shame ourselves and others.

We boast to get "likes" for what we think people want to hear or see. The in-your-face smiling selfies, perfect homes, extraordinary happiness, the sunshine, and rainbows that pour out of our asses; it can all be a bit overwhelming. If you are currently not happy in life, social media makes it so hard not to feel shameful when you look at how "perfect" other people's lives are.

Now along with self-doubt, you have a heavy load of shame because of the societal pressures to appear a certain way. Eventually, you will end up in a sad, low, depressing energy of loneliness where everything feels impossible. You have become a prisoner of Modern Fear, once shame, doubt, and toxicity causes you to start comparing yourself to others.

Shame is a trap within the critical mind. It prevents us from accessing our feelings and depletes our worthiness. To release ourselves from shame is a practice of witnessing the greatness that only exists within our own self.

SUFFERING

The pain that you experience is real, it is unique to you, and there is no denying its presence; however, the **mental suffering you endure is a choice.**

Our mental suffering is a response to our pain or discomfort. When we are suffering, we are more susceptible to the influence of h*te. Misery loves company, and as we lash out from our suffering and wish harm on others, we are holding ourselves within an invisible prison of Modern Fear. This wish of harm sends frequencies of disharmony into your existence.

At some point in your life, you will have a thought that is born out of anger, frustration, sadness, or disappointment. You will hope for some sort of suffering to another or yourself. We all do it, we are human, and it is a natural defense of the mind. We can feel justified, an eye for an eye, but we are not. You will be the one that suffers the karmic consequences of these intentions.

If you are hoping or are programmed to expect bad things, then you should do some investigative work to find the source of your pain, being gentle with yourself by using love, compassion, and understanding. None of us are meant to suffer.

MONEY

My history with money is one of my most significant and most painful teachers. Growing up poor made me believe that money was the root of all evil. I always wanted money to be around, yet every time it came into my life, I couldn't get rid of it fast enough, either through spending on myself or generosity to others. I used to have a love-hate relationship with money, now I respect the fact that money opens up opportunities and it doesn't have to be at the hand of greed, but instead can be through the influence of generosity.

Mainstream entertainment does an excellent job portraying lifestyles with money: big houses, fancy cars, and exotic trips around the world. The people and characters that are featured in entertainment typically have an abundance of money, although this could be a façade as well.

Entertainment is a form of marketing, and marketing is designed to influence your feelings of persuasion directly. Marketing is a form of manipulation and doesn't require truth, do not be fooled.

Scarcity mindset is a trick and a manipulation of our decadent social culture; it is incredibly easy to fall prey to this vibration and become attuned to Modern Fear. I know because I once lived in it. I once was on the path of survival, and the lack of money caused stress to the point that it overwhelmed all other feelings.

What is a scarcity mindset? It is the thought pattern that you NEED "something," and there is just not enough of that "something." This "something" is typically money because money is the currency that our society currently trades for food, water, shelter, safety, and all the extra bonuses of leisure and luxury.

Does scarcity feel familiar to you? Are you living paycheck to paycheck, with no savings and an excessive amount of debt, entirely in denial or unconscious with your relationship around money? I will raise my hand. I am guilty of the above, truth is truth, and once I admitted it, it was like turning on the facet to receiving abundance. I had to wake up to the fact that the debt I thought I was leveraging was me spending beyond my means and holding me in slavery to the lender.

The stress of money is fear, and fear is repellent to the abundant, fluid energetics of money. **If you blame money for your worries in life, you are repelling money.**

Money is a made-up currency. The only value that money has is the value we place on it. You do not need to worship or lust after money to attract it into your life; however, you do need to have some respect for the benefits that money brings. Again I ask you, what is your relationship with money?

Money is like love, it feels good when you have it, and when you don't, you know something is missing.

> *"Some people are so poor, all they have is money."*
> *Bob Marley*

I have met plenty of sad, lonely people who have struck it rich financially; however, what money does not buy is an authentic human connection. Rich or poor, we all crave relationships of the heart.

Are you a person who has an abundance of money? How do you pay forward your success? Do you care about sharing the wealth?

Financially secure people are either born into it or have worked for it. Either way, if you are economically secure, impressive! What's next? How do you plan to inspire the world with the generosity of your prosperity?

Generosity is attractive energy for money. It says to the universe: "My cup is full and I can give. I am not afraid of scarcity. I have plenty, and so shall you."

On the other end of the spectrum, financially insecure people, meaning either that money is scarce or they are fully leveraged, have many reasons for ending up there. No matter how you got there, it sucks. I can personally attest to that. I will never forget what it feels like to be hungry because of having no money to buy food, the bottomless pit deep in my stomach, the mental confusion as to why the cabinets were empty.

The baseline necessity of life is about meeting survival needs (shelter, food, utilities), not the quality of how you want to live. Survival is the difference between thriving and death. The only two certainties in your experience are your birth and your death; how life plays out in between is the adventure and is often directly attached to the amount of money that will flow through your life.

I spent my youth in poverty and the hard life that comes along with it, where everyone was trying to compete for limited resources. There were never enough resources available when living within scarcity and poverty. Anything that I got was taking away from someone else. My probation officer at fifteen years old said it best, "Society does not want people like you to succeed." This was a pivotal moment in my life. I knew he was right. Whatever I was going to accomplish was going to be on me. I knew that I didn't want to be poor. I knew I needed to figure out this money game because every time I had to see my probation officer and pay my restitution, it was a reminder that I worked hard for my money. And yet, there I was, paying for my criminal behaviors. More importantly, I wanted to prove society wrong, which was a core driver for me at the beginning of my journey of self-improvement.

As a side note, it is not my current belief that it does any good to prove someone else wrong. I now practice intentional listening so that I may contribute and expand with someone else's experience, rather than trying to control or outdo them.

One of the most detrimental beliefs about being in a good relationship with money is that money does not matter. There are plenty of people making the declaration that money doesn't matter to them. They believe money shouldn't influence them because they don't want to be corrupted and fall victim to the influence of greed. This is a lie and a Modern Fear, as these people are afraid of the way money or the lack thereof makes them feel. If you are part of mainstream society, then money should matter to you, as it is required to participate in life, to pay for the roof over your head, put food on your table and have adventures.

Money is not evil. Only people who misuse the power of money are evil. **Money is a tool.**

*"There is no shame in making money.
The shame in life is not helping others."
Jeff Hoffman*

Money provides security, and therefore money most assuredly should matter to you. You deserve to have security in life, and you deserve to have comfort, which money can provide.

What are your relationship with money and your financial spending? If you are a shopaholic and are spending money just to fill a void within yourself, then you are experiencing an emotional betrayal with your spending. It feels good to shop, fill your cart, and check out; however, when you get home and realize you bought something remarkably similar to something you already have, it deflates the good feeling. This habit is costing you your precious time, energy, and money, and for what? A cluttered home?

As a consumer, you vote with your dollars. Suppose you are addicted to shopping, and you are giving all your money over to big box stores that have shelves filled with products made by companies that only care about getting your hard-earned dollars, not about the products you put on or in your body and home. In that case, the money energy you are aligning with is not of the highest vibration.

I would like to take a moment here and acknowledge the movement toward sacred and heart economy. Some forward-thinking individuals understand that our energy is our only real currency. When you know that your energy and time are your most valuable asset, you can start to exchange differently with others.

We all exchange our time and energy for money. I understand the power behind what we do with money. I believe we all have a moral obligation to become more aware of the impact of our dollars. I choose to consume or purchase now with my heart, I support small and local businesses as much as possible, and the greatest gift to this spending philosophy is the connected relationships I get to make with the people who are receiving my money.

I consciously choose how my dollars are spent. I try my hardest not to spend money at chain stores. I avoid products that I know are bad for the environment. I will not spend my money on "food" that I know is poisoning us as humans. I try my hardest to shop locally as much as possible.

For example, there is a restaurant in town called Green Source; if you ever come to visit Missoula, I thoroughly recommend this spot. I love this restaurant because the source of the food matters, which supports and serves the community because they purchase their produce, and there is a lot of produce from local farmers as much as possible. I know that when I spend money within their establishment, I am supporting my local community, and that feels good. This is a very different experience than if I were to go through the drive-through at a chain fast-food restaurant, where I have no idea where the food comes from and my money going towards an industry that is getting rich off making humans sick. If you haven't watched Super-Size Me, enough said, take a couple of hours of your life and learn how detrimental this "food" is for your body.

If you do not have a conscious and active relationship with money, odds are it's probably stressing you out with mental worry and causing you to become physically dis-eased with upset stomachs, headaches, or insomnia. You are becoming sick as you deny the potential of the powerful tool money can be. Understandably, you don't want to feel a connection to money because of the stress. Money becomes something that you curse as our society forces its existence, while at the same time, it is something you need. Your money magic is trapped in Modern Fear.

But what if money felt good to you?

To shift my feelings around money from bad to good, I started to imagine all of the generous things I could do for myself, others, and my community. It gave money a new life and a new purpose for me. It made me excited about having more money in my life.

CHASING THE AMERICAN DREAM

We are told as Americans that there is an equality of opportunity, allowing for our highest aspirations to be achieved. The American Dream goes back to the creation of the Declaration of Independence, where it states, "all men are created equal." The entrepreneurship of so many Americans has carried this dream, and it is an illusion for most. There is no equality in poverty and hardship. Americans are stacked against each other in their pursuit of the top.

From my personal experience, I do believe the dream can be real for some people that are entirely driven and do not get easily discouraged; however, I think this type of individual is more of an outlier than the norm.

By the definition of The American Dream, I have made it.

I live in a humble home situated on an acre of land, deep in the woods of the Sapphire Mountain Range. I live a fairytale life, with my prince charming, two magical boxer friends, and birds singing most of the year through. The pace of my life is slow enough that I enjoy daily walks in the woods and can get lost in contemplation while watching the clouds pass overhead. I work an extremely secure, well-paying job. I have less debt and more savings than the average American.

I can remember as a child, sitting on my bed, dreaming of having a secure home, food to eat, and if I could only be successful when I grew up, life would be perfect; by all definitions of "perfect," I am pretty dang close.

The American Dream can work. I know this for a fact. However, it is a rigged game that benefits the few and requires the energy of the many. The American Dream is attached to the puppet strings of those at the top. Dangling carrots for those at the bottom to chase. Greed is a driving force within the American Dream, often leading to the corruption of those who have achieved. At the same time, they continue to make exorbitant amounts of money off the backs of the lower socioeconomic working class.

We see a great divide between the people who have and the people who have not. This spread has led to a culture of injustice for those who do not have. The greed of one creates scarcity for another, and scarcity is a prison cell of Modern Fear. The use of power to dominate or control others is a form of modern slavery, as oppressed individuals fall victim to controlling industries.

A long time ago, lords of the land understood that holding their people to taxation and financially burdening others was a way to keep them imprisoned to their rulings. Rights and liberties were tied to the ability to meet taxation requirements. This is the moment when the misuse of money energy began. It was stolen from the masses and controlled by the few. The security of home became attached to the ability to pay.

Today, large institutions understand that holding the masses in fear of money is a way to control us. The traditional approach to the American Dream was to put society through the conformity funnel.

Ever since the industrial revolution and the increased need for more workers, our society has funneled us through a channel that puts us into a system that mostly benefits those on top. This order of serving those on top is widely accepted by the masses, as there is less risk involved with feeding the dream of someone else than forging ahead and building your own dream. We are trained from a young age to attend school through an outdated educational model, which is systematically designed to get us into the habit of dedicating the majority of our waking hours to work. This perpetuates an illusion of choice and equality within the American Dream.

Once we graduate from the educational system, we are directed into the achievement of what corporations define as success, competing against our peers for the "good job." We join the rat-race and see who comes out on top. Some people are going to understand the game of this organization quickly and will climb to the top. However, the majority are going to be worker bees, going into the JOB every day for nothing more than a paycheck to pay the debt that we have accumulated.

I got trapped in this cycle early on in my life.

I moved out of my mother's house when I was sixteen years old. I furnished my apartment with items from "Rent to Own," which was the beginning of **the habit of borrowing money** so that I could appear to be accomplished. Then, leveraging debt was the only way I could figure out how to get out of the lower-income bracket. This in itself is a delusion; filling my home with items that I didn't own and paying high interest on the terms did not remove me from a lower income. It held me there. The people in the lowest socioeconomic class are subject to the highest interest rates, which consist of entirely unethical terms and conditions attached to borrowing money. It is a fixed system to keep people enslaved to the lenders.

Are you the person that lives a lifestyle that appears financially successful, but everything is leveraged?

Culturally, it is acceptable to have our cars obtained through a payment plan (leased or owned). Our experiences and shopping habits are paid through credit cards. Consumerism is an addictive behavior, and as such, we are programmed to shop. We are taught the "power" of our credit score and the money shuffle. We are transferring debt from one creditor to the next, just to keep up with the payments. I know this because I have been caught in this cycle my whole life. If this feels familiar, then you, my friend, are imprisoned in Modern Fear and are a slave to the lender, being shackled by interest.

The stress of debt keeps you up at night, and you're working to pay bills on things that have already become old. You have no real strategy of paying the debt off until the loan is amortized, or you are able to transfer it to a lower interest credit card. **These behaviors, connected to consumer debt, are consuming YOU from the inside out.**

For twenty years, I was a severe workaholic, chasing the money that I did not have so I could buy food and pay for shelter, which provided safety and security; additionally, it allowed for all the gluttonous decadence that I could swing. My workaholic tendency blinded my ability to see the drawbacks and physical stress of accumulating too much debt and trying to make ends meet.

I thought I was winning at the game until I recognized that I was actually trapped inside of it.

To live in debt to something or someone gives away your power. You might feel in control because you are able to pay your bills, but what about savings? Do you have any? What happens if the proverbial shit hits the fan?

How secure are you really?

If your financial "freedom" is connected to your ability to borrow money, you do not have freedom. You have an obligation of repayment to someone else. You have the stress of a bill that is due and, if not paid on time, has additional financial penalties.

Do you have a habit of living outside of your means to appear aligned with modern-day pop culture? This is an invisible prison of Modern Fear. Choices you make that build debt through institutions hold you, prisoner, to products and items that quickly lose their value. Everything can be financed these days; however, by the time you actually own the product, it is old, and you are ready for a "new" or "updated" replacement. This cycle is incredibly damaging, especially if you have "shiny new things syndrome."

There is an extreme difference between living impoverished and living in abundance. Don't let the false illusions of luxury lure you into trapping yourself into more debt. Step back just a few steps and meet yourself where you currently are. Lifestyles don't leap from poor to rich. There are many steps in between. The first step is, to be honest with yourself and decide where you want to go from here.

If you are leveraged, have minimal savings, and your debt-to-income ratio is high, **stop spending**. Evaluate your lifestyle and start making proactive decisions to change your behaviors around money.

There are many financial planning theories out there. If you are just starting to think about money and making it work for you rather than you working for money, I recommend Dave Ramsey's approach. His method is attainable for **anyone** that can be disciplined and dedicated to the motto: "Live now like no one else, so later you can live like no one else."

Another important thing to keep in mind is that the cost of money can be high. To make money, you must invest your time. If you are not making money and you are borrowing someone else's money, your cost is the interest attached to the loan. What is the actual cost of the spending habits that you have in your life? Have you amortized your debt and looked at the finance charges associated with your loans and credit cards? If you haven't done the research, it is clearly pointed out on your credit card statements. The financial cost of interest should be evaluated.

Because we accumulate debt, we put most of our energy into our job, which prevents us from knowing what drives our passion.

What lights your fire? I can tell you that spending endless hours in front of a computer screen, sitting in a cubicle, does nothing for my fire. I want to be in a deep, intimate connection with real human beings who are on a quest to discover the deeper meaning of their life.

What do you want in life? It feels scary and incredibly vulnerable to admit and ask for what it is we truly desire; it goes against what society has habitually trained us to do through the conformity funnel, designed to feed the success of corporations and not the success of individuals.

What's the point of your job? Perhaps it is the security of the paycheck, or maybe it is your true passion and purpose in life. As I worked my way up through corporate America, my dedication to my job was about having security. There is not a lot of risk with a job if you are willing to conform and submit to the rules and culture of the company. However, this is only true as long as the economy stays healthy, which as a global culture, we humans have been shown how truly fragile this infrastructure is. The COVID-19 pandemic proved that jobs could quickly be taken away if the business is forced to close. There is no financial sovereignty when your livelihood is dependent upon a paycheck.

In my achievement of stability and safety through my job, my soul's purpose started to feel stagnant, and a new quest began for me, seeking a deeper meaning to life connected to the support of love.

Stability, safety, love, and support are everything that I am looking for in life. Yet, I know that statement is not entirely true because I have all of those feelings in my life now, AND I am still seeking to impact and influence the world to feel more deeply. I am realizing right now that in accomplishing my goal of the American Dream, I failed to define a more meaningful mission and purpose for my existence. I did everything that society said I was supposed to do in school and work, and yet something was lacking.

That was until I found my spiritual Source.

I was deep in the rural hillsides of Puerto Rico at an Alternavida Retreat, connecting more deeply to my inner vulnerabilities, and the next activity was a group shamanic journey. Paco, the Shaman, gave one direction, then he walked right up to me, tapped me directly on my third eye, and said, "Home."

When the drumming started, home is where I went.

In a subconscious, deeply relaxed, dangerously curious state of being, I am confident that my soul left my physical body and traveled through light-years of time, weaving and sprinting back to the moment of its beginning. While in that space of time, surrounded by a gentle glowing light, I felt at home, and for the first time, I knew where I belonged. I genuinely have no words to describe that state of euphoria. At its essence is a knowing within my soul that I am part of something larger than my human existence can ever fully comprehend.

When Paco started to recall the group from their journey, my soul did not want to leave its home. I felt complete and at peace, and there was no desire to return, yet my body was fighting to bring it back.

Physically, I was experiencing what felt like an earthquake in my chest. I could feel the invisible prison around my heartbreaking apart, and it was agonizing. I was experiencing heartbreak. My soul did not want to come back to its body. I believe now that it was my soul's heart that broke that day. Within my knowing, my soul understood that it must release its peace so that my body could go on living. At that moment in time, it felt like a sacrifice of the first moment of true peace in my life.

The return into my body felt like I was on a roller coaster that was being flushed down a toilet in a chaotic, terrifying fashion. My body was sweating profusely. In the distance, I could hear people in the room singing, so I used their voices to navigate my return. When I opened my eyes for the first time, everything was a blur. I was told that they appeared to be vacant. The second time I opened my eyes, I was able to start to focus, and what I saw was true love hanging over my body. My friends were sitting over me, looks of relief and tears streaming down their faces. They, too, knew that I had left, and this was my return to the home of my body.

That day, I, my soul, was bathed in the light of my Source. I indeed met my God self and was given the gift of the wisdom that truly we are all one. There is no separation from you and me, from God and Self, there is only the illusion of our individualism.

When I left Puerto Rico, I could no longer deny a more meaningful existence, which I felt had abandoned me for so much of my life. Upon my return to Seattle and the mundane of the American Dream, chasing status rather than purpose, I quickly accepted that my world was going to evolve into something with more meaning and deeper connection into myself and with others.

Our desperation of individualization, which is a paradigm of fear, putting us into survival mode, has stretched and torn us apart into a society that doesn't care for each other. We have been brainwashed to believe that our individual success is more important than the collective wellbeing. This pressure to do everything on our own is a considerable burden upon our collective shoulders. We culturally don't have the energy to care for each other very much anymore. We are exhausted from life. We have been tricked into overloading ourselves. However, I feel that there is potential hope coming with a cultural shift towards caring for each other. We are witnessing a beautiful movement as Americans are coming together, demanding reform around the injustice of police brutality and the corruption within the criminal justice system.

The experience of life is so much bigger than the American Dream; yes, it is a path that can fill your material life and potentially something more; however, it is only one path, and there are so many more to choose.

I ask you this, and I invite you to stop here and feel this question. **What do you care about? And I mean really care.** The kind of care that is scary. The type of care that feels vulnerable. The kind of care that is wrapped up with love. I genuinely care about the human experience we all get to have, and I want everyone to have the chance to feel safety, stability, and security. The old systems are broken and need to be updated to match who we are today, and not who we were during the time of our country's founding fathers.

What matters most to you?

Frequently, it takes a huge life event like death, cancer, or bankruptcy to find the heart of the above question. The American Dream pushes us to focus on the quantity of achievement rather than the quality of life. When we are focused on the quantity, we lose quality because the value doesn't matter as much and can be replaced. When we invert this and focus on the quality, the necessity of quantity disappears because we value what we have.

In the contemplation of what matters most to me, never once does the American Dream or money come into my thoughts; instead, it is always a living relationship; my friends, my family, my partner, my dogs, my sisters... MY OWN LIFE.

It took me living in the woods surrounded by breathtaking mountains, living next to a running river, escaping the reality of city life, and spending an insane amount of time alone in silence, for me to learn just how important my own life is. And how it is the one life that I need to care about the most.

Self-care is hard work. PERIOD. Learning to give me space to feel, allowing for all parts of myself to be witnessed and honored; this was a long valley through the shadows of myself.

Chasing the American Dream sends so many of us into burnout; instead of prioritizing the nurturance of our being, we put external demands of success in front of everything else. Self-care is a decision that has to be made every single day: we either self-care, or we don't.

How do you take care of yourself?

When do you think about self-care? I can promise if you are stressed-out over money, you either never think about self-care, or you think about it all the time because you know life is meant to feel better than it does.

We are living in a time when it feels too hard to care for ourselves because we are mentally and emotionally exhausted from the demands of life. Because we are not caring for ourselves, we feel awful, compounding the effects of the exhaustion. Talk about being stuck between a rock and a hard place, something is going to break, and it is you.

The cultural demands of making money, along with the desire to live a life full of purpose, can create an enormous amount of pressure as we strive to meet our expectations. I broke under this pressure, so I know this to be true. I expected myself to achieve a dream that was given to me by society, rather than living a dream that was driven by my soul's purpose. The lack of connection to my desires and broken relationship with money committed me to a path that was not fulfilling on many levels.

Many tools are available to change your relationship with money. I can only speak to my journey and the desire to step beyond the American Dream and change my relationship with money. To learn to accept that I too deserve to receive the security of money, I need to be disciplined to the fact that I don't want to be enslaved to debt or dependent upon other systems for my food. I had to stop the pattern of instant gratification, and instead focus my intention on the outcome of sovereignty that I seek, which is in alignment with my soul's purpose.

THE SHAME OF SCARCENESS

Personally, when finances are tight, I start to shame myself regarding money. Questioning, how did I let myself get into this position? I doubt my capacity to provide security for myself, and I can't even imagine what the pressure of this shame would feel like if I were to have mouths to feed.

Does the shame of not having enough money cause you to doubt yourself? Do you feel shame attached to lacking money? Do you have thoughts like, "I can't provide." "I barely get by." "How am I going to pay my bills?"

Is it money you want, or is it the security that comes along with the money that you desire?

I was ashamed of being poor when I was a child. Think about this: as a child, I had no control over the economic status of my environment, and yet I still felt shame. Poverty is my historical fact, unchangeable, and was outside of my control from birth.

My mom did her best, but we were poor. We were on governmental assistance, bouncing from home to home, school to school, going anywhere that we could find support either through people, organizations, or work. We experienced homelessness, lived in trailer parks filled with drug addicts, and struggled to meet our basic survival needs.

In response to my shame, I tried to hide being poor. I lied about the toys that I received at holiday times. I would have "friends" drop me off miles from where I lived so they wouldn't know and generally masqueraded through my childhood by pretending to be someone with status, which I was not. I never felt my value or my worthiness because I was too concerned with how others saw me. This pattern of behavior prevented me from ever letting others get too close to me.

I judged myself for us not having money before I let others judge me. I knew I was different and believed if others knew, they would treat me differently. I created my own invisible prison of shame to try to protect

LEAH LOVELIGHT MICHAEL | 91

myself from others' abuse by abusing myself first. This behavior created reactive anxiety around money that ruled my life from childhood to adulthood.

In my confusion of Modern Fear, money was the root of all hardship. I judged people with money. I judged people without money. I knew money didn't feel "right" to me, as it made me feel weak and vulnerable to others. I was trapped between not wanting to be poor and not wanting to be financially successful, which I thought automatically meant greed. My wants held me, prisoner. I made enough money to appear comfortable, achieving this appearance through the financing of debt or the credit card shuffle.

Modern Fear around money is complicated. To many people, money does not feel safe, which comes from the idea that money is evil, corruptible, and can easily lead to greed. The belief that you do not deserve money and the façade of pretending to have money decreases the value of money and the tool it can be in your life.

To get freedom from my doubts around money and the reactive anxiety that I felt towards wealth required that I go inside myself. Modern Fear was attached to the socioeconomic status of my youth. I consciously went on a quest to find the little girl imprisoned in moments around shame and money. A memory that surfaced was of a time when I was young, and a friend came over wanting to play with a toy that I had lied about receiving. I had to tell my friend that it broke, and we threw it away. I was always lying because I was afraid of being rejected. I had no attachment to what my value was because my external world reflected hardship.

You cannot fix the problems you have today if you do not accept them in your past.

Self-healing money shame requires a change in belief, a shift in the frequency of your feelings, and the establishment of a new reality. Our value is not dependent upon the amount of money we have in the bank. It is attached to the quality of our presence. Rewire the old story that you have been telling yourself. The old story is the warden of your prison. It is the construction of Modern Fear. To get out, you must be willing to receive the new story of freedom.

To create an empowered money story takes time. To release an old thought, behavior, or emotional pattern, you must dedicate yourself to consciously recognizing when you are in the old story again, rather than committed to the new story. For example, I have established a daily practice of looking at my checking account, as I want to have a loving relationship with my money, and I know when I avoid looking online, I am slipping back into my old story. I can feel the fear rising within me. I begin to worry that there is not enough. I imagine looking and nothing being there, and sometimes nothing is, and that is okay. At least I am fully conscious of my money and not in avoidance of the truth.

I've released, and honestly am still releasing, Modern Fear around money. I began by visiting my youthful self in my mind, visualizing my adult self holding the little girl I once was, and I affirmed to her that being poor as a kid was okay. I told her, "When you grow up, nobody is going to care. You are awesome, and you are disciplined, and you do the work. You always have food in your fridge. You are no longer poor."

This mental practice has supported me in releasing my shame around money because I can assure myself that we, me, and my younger self, do have the security and safety that money can provide now. I have repeated this practice more times than I can count. It takes effort to forgive truly and to rewire old stories, especially ones as painful and deep as shame.

To accept your history with an open heart is not easy work. To allow forgiveness as an adult is hard. Both are needed to get freedom from the emotional prisons that you created as a kid to protect yourself.

This work of releasing the shame around scarceness opens you up to the feelings of the potential abundance that is readily available to you.

THE PITY PARTY

I am a raving fan of the pity party. It is best done in isolation and darkness. I mean, I really get into it. I recognize pity's presence, and I allow space for it to be. I acknowledge the lower vibrations and self-talk. I put on my comfy clothes and crawl into bed so that I can disappear. I let my sadness spill out through my tears. I numb my attention, mindlessly watching Netflix until I pass out.

Once I wake up to a new day, I try again. The pity isn't allowed to linger. I simply let my sadness to take over for a short period, to be expressed, and then it is time to reclaim that energy and rewire it for something greater.

It isn't always this easy to get out of a pity party.

The doubt that is created in the feeling of sadness is heavy energy. The most straightforward task of getting out of bed can become impossible. When opportunities of something more exciting are offered, you think, "I don't have the energy for that," and decline the potential escape from the pity party. I know that if I leave the party and do something else, I almost always feel better, yet I often choose to stay in the heaviness because joy actually sounds harder than pity.

Sadness causes the brain to be foggy, preventing you from being able to process what is best for you right now. This fogginess keeps us blind from seeing anything that might help us, and in fact, it attracts energies that can drag us further into the pity.

Sadness is a feeling that can be traced back to fear. Sadness originates from within, and even if the world is saying yes, sadness might only hear no. We lose our capability to see beyond the hardship, and if solutions are offered or presented, there is no receiving them. These "helping" hands create more annoyance and despair because the expectation from the "helpers" is too much to handle when we are in a lower vibration. The offers can set us up to feel like we are disappointing others. Heavier feelings, like isolation, segregation, and doubt, focus our attention inside. They make it hard to let in positive opportunities. There is no logic within the pity party. It is nothing but a delusional disco. The Self lost within the Self.

Pity parties bring questions like, "Why does this only happen to me?" This type of question causes us to fall into victim energy, compounding the effect of the pity party.

Every pity party has an underlying fear; I am not cared for, I am not worthy, I am not understood, or I am not appreciated.

When you don't express your feelings, especially one as strong as sadness, you are telling yourself that it is easier to ignore fear than it is to hear fear. Let me rephrase; it becomes easier to let fear push you into an invisible prison of sadness rather than to fight for your existence on the outside of it.

Have a pity party. I encourage it. However, set a timer to limit and honor the pity and then move forward.

DEATH

Death is inevitable. It is a cycle that is always repeating in harmony with birth. In nature, we watch the spring flowers bloom and wither away in the fall. We watch rushing rivers become dry river beds. We watch our grandparents pass, and babies are born.

We fear the death of others because losing something that we love is painful. We fear the death of ourselves because that is the end of this life.

Most people are afraid of death because what is beyond is unknown. Your belief and faith might promise an afterlife, or you might believe that this life right now is all you get.

Death brings with it many feelings: denial, guilt, anger, depression, pain, and, eventually, acceptance. Each of you will deal with death in your own way. The sadness that comes with death should be felt and not buried. Mourning death, letting the release flow through you, will bring with it unexpected gifts. Suppressing your emotions around death and grief will keep you trapped within Modern Fear, and this will have consequential ripples throughout your life.

Death entering into my life created the greatest opportunity for me to connect to how I was living.

Time is short, and it is our most scarce resource.

Every decision you make will either shorten or extend the time that is your existence. If you never think about death, then you are never thinking about the consequences of how you are living, and life-shortening habits are not that big of a deal. However, if you love life and you don't want to die too quickly, then living a life of well-being might be beneficial to you.

We can easily get lost in the sadness of death. After all, it feels like a piece of you is missing. I will invite you here to change perceptions. Shift your focus to what you gained in life because of the person who has passed. Celebrate and appreciation as much as possible. This acknowledgment and honoring keeps the person's spirit closer to you. Each person comes into

96 | MODERN FEAR: THE INVISIBLE PRISON

our life for a reason, a season, or a lifetime. It is up to you to determine the effects that a person's passing will bear upon your world. I hope that it is one of love.

JUDGEMENTAL BEHAVIORS

"Who are you to judge the life I live? I know I'm not perfect -and I don't live to be- but before you start pointing fingers... make sure your hands are clean!"
Bob Marley

Please keep in mind; this entire section is my judgment and opinion. Being judgmental, by definition, means having or displaying an **excessively critical** point of view.

Are you, or do you know someone who you believe to be, judgmental? Of course, you do. We all can be critical to varying degrees. The effects of judgment, be that of others or yourself, are detrimental to your energetic life force and increase reactive anxiety. This tendency is your own toxicity showing.

Judgmental tendencies can be expressed by body language, the crossing of your arms, or the sneer on your face or the skeptical tone of your voice and the disagreeing words that you use.

Judgment exists in your head, polluting your thoughts and self-respect. This mostly happens when we are in a state of comparison to others, or if we are not meeting our own expectations.

Most often, judgments are overheard directed toward other people, and our society soaks up every last cruel word as if it were completely acceptable.

You know you are judging when you hear yourself say:
- "I would never do ..."
- "I can't believe that ..."
- "It is unacceptable to ... "
- "What were you thinking?"

Judgmental behavior sets others apart from you as a form of comparison. They are often expressed with negativity, creating a "better than" situation, preventing you from being able to view alternative perspectives.

Judgmental negativity increases anxiety. As the doom and gloom build, the anxiety becomes more reactive, leading to increased stress, which is a symptom of Modern Fear.

I am sure some of you are feeling resistance in this section, perhaps even getting defensive towards my self-declared judgments, and that is okay. We are all entitled to an opinion.

Webster defines an opinion as a view or judgment formed about something, not necessarily based on fact or knowledge. Opinions are subjective to the individual. Opinions can become harmful when emotionally charged and do not have a purpose-designed for the greater good. You can choose if you want to project this dangerous opinion forward; however, you will be the one that suffers from this projection.

Your opinions are a direct result of the experiences of your life. They are based on your beliefs, and as such, opinions can evolve.

Opinions are individualistic. They vary from you to me. This book is based on my observations throughout my life and the views that I have formed. This book does not make me right or wrong; it only presents me as an authority on Modern Fear because of my experiences.

The person you are today might not feel the same as the person you were yesterday. Life happens in the moment. As much as the moments seem to be predictable, there is always a level of uncertainty. Life-changing experiences happen quickly. They are sudden and often take a bit of time to process and understand the altogether effect they have on you.

It is crucial to observe your excessively critical opinions, also known as judgments. Energetically, these judgments are immensely heavy and rigid; they often create blocks and can be extremely draining on our life force. The value of our worth is often tied up in our judgments, which is why it is important to keep them in check.

It is easy to get caught up in comparison. Social media and mass entertainment provide plenty to which we can compare ourselves. We see people who "appear" to have their lives together; however, in truth, they can be completely broken on the inside. Your life is uniquely yours. You cannot be or have someone else's life. We each get to have our very own human experience.

When you find yourself being extra critical or judgmental, just be honest with yourself. Think about removing yourself from the experience and practice being a witness. See yourself or the other person that is being critical, and notice how it feels to experience that criticalness. This practice removes the charged reactive stimulation, allowing space for you to pause in observation, rather than react from the critical mind. Witnessing and observing are proactive tools for replacing judgmental opinions.

When we interact with one another, practice kindness, and try not to devalue another's opinion too quickly. We must try to meet the world with an open mind, centered heart, and a respectful approach. Delivery matters and is based on intentions. There is a line between hard opinions and opinions that are hard to hear. Be careful of the judgmental barb.

The more you become connected to your thoughts, feelings, and your own body, the quicker you will be able to acknowledge when you are expressing a harmful, judgmental perspective. This book is an opportunity for you to stop and reflect. Ask yourself why you feel like you are in the position to be the judge and jury of others.

The more you practice observation, the more your energetic tension will decrease, and slowly you will be released from the invisible prison of Modern Fear.

I used to judge myself for lack of money and where I grew up. I used to judge myself for all the trauma that happened to me. During my healing journey and working with the tool of witnessing myself and my experiences, I have been able to shift those judgments into acceptance and kindness. I can have compassion for myself now that I practice releasing my judgments.

DISHONESTY

How honest are you? I bet just now you answered that question, "pretty honest." Which, in reality, might be the biggest lie we tell ourselves. The brain is a master storyteller, designed to keep us safe and comfortable. It subjectively filters the world through your personal lens and can eliminate facts or details that might exist. My older sister has shared a memory of walking into her kitchen and seeing me sweeping the ceiling; I have no recollection of that moment, so for me, it is hard to believe, and yet for her, that story is true.

Imagination and curiosity are two of the greatest gifts we are given as humans. These two attributes open the door for all of the magic we get to create in life. Pretending can be used as a tool in the law of attraction to develop the life that we want. I have used pretending, by telling myself, "I am a published author," for years. Sometimes, this pretending has driven me to work diligently on this book, like I am right now. Sometimes, this pretending was only words because the action was missing, which ultimately led to self-shaming for not honoring my word to myself.

For the most part, pretending is an act of dreaming. However, it can also have an element of lying. There is a fine line between pretending and lying if the malicious intention is behind the pretending.

Lying is a practiced behavior, and it starts when we are young. We all can admit when we got our hand caught in the cookie jar; we would still deny the fact that we did it because of the fear of getting in trouble. Lying starts as a defense mechanism.

Here is my truth, one that I am not sure you would expect to read. I have been a liar; at least part of me was anyway. I tell you this not because I want to cause you to question my honesty, but because I can't ask you to evaluate this part of yourself without disclosing the dishonesty within me. I feel like this behavior is part of what makes us human. We can influence and manipulate reality. We are the conscious creators of our existence, and

LEAH LOVELIGHT MICHAEL | 101

whether you are active or passive in that creation is up to you.

I started lying to myself at a young age. I was so good at lying that I would forget and block out horrific things that happened to me. I lost track of where the truth ended, and the lie began. One of the top survival skills I developed early on was being a chameleon. I am a master at walking into a room and disappearing or fitting in. I lied as a youth to everyone, not because I had an evil character, but because of the shame, I felt due to where I came from and what happened to me. I was ashamed of my truth, so I made up lies, wanting to be accepted rather than feeling tossed aside by society.

Our thoughts control our reality. Our words define our world, and our actions dictate what we manifest.

We lie for the simplest of reasons, to justify our actions, to avoid responsibility, to hide what we fear others will use against us, or to fit in simply. Lying can become a habit and a completely unconscious practice.

The real warning here isn't necessarily about lying to others. It is about lying to ourselves. How many times have you said, I am not going to do something, but you did. How many times have you said you are going to do something, but you didn't? Each time we make these declarations to ourselves, and we do not follow through, we are crippling our ability to be able to trust ourselves by not honoring our word.

When we consciously manipulate the truth, we are strategically lying; this conscious practice works for a lot of people. If you have ever been in the presence of a manipulator, they have become so good at strategic lying that it has become a subconscious habit. It is now part of their energetic makeup.

If we do not practice intentional presence with our truth, our entire existence can easily play out in a tale of subtle lies.

One of the biggest lies I hear regularly is, "It doesn't matter." When I listen to people share sorrows about a person they love who has hurt them, they will almost always try to jump out of the heartache by claiming, "It doesn't matter, what's done is done." They brush away what feels essential and hide behind a completely untrue phrase.

You matter. I matter. We matter, and everything associated matters, because LIFE MATTERS. Claiming that something doesn't "matter" devalues your energy and prevents you from being able to reclaim the

102 | MODERN FEAR: THE INVISIBLE PRISON

energy that is stuck within the experience that "doesn't matter." Your energy is your life force, and so it matters. It is our responsibility to allow our truths to flow so that our energy does not become stagnant or blocked.

If you are avoiding your feelings or lying to yourself about the way you feel, you are trapped in Modern Fear. Subtle dishonesty is likely all around you. This is a hard truth and heavy awakening to come to, and one that should be approached with gentle finesse.

The shame of admitting to being a liar, or dishonesty (if you want a more gentle word), is a beast! When I first realized my truth and consciously committed to being an honest person, I had to look back to recognize all the lies I was told and telling. It made me feel like a piece of poop. There is no other way to describe it because I always thought of myself as an honest person. This perhaps was the biggest lie I was telling myself.

Conscious action was required on my part to rewire the pattern of dishonesty; I am not perfect, and old habits die hard. I am always catching myself. If you have ever had a conversation with me, or if you ever listen to me talk, I promise that you will hear, "Wait, that is not true," as I will quickly fall on the sword and admit the truth. I value honesty, transparency, and authenticity, and thinking, and speaking truth requires absolute devotion on my part to living in alignment.

When I was living within dishonesty, I was living in constant fear of the truth being discovered. I worried what people would think if they discovered I was lying. This prevented me from having fully connected relationships with others.

Integrity, which encompasses honesty, is one of my core values, which allows me to feel a sense of freedom because it gives me a moral compass to follow. This isn't true for everyone. We each have our driving forces. During my self-work and expansion with my spirituality and universal connection, I quickly learned that what we give, we receive. When I was lying to myself on the inside, my world reflected dishonesty on the outside. When I made the conscious decision to align with integrity on the inside, the deception within my external reality started to slip away, and I now experience deeper connections with others who want to live in the same integrity and alignment as I do.

SELFISH TO SELFLESS

As individuals, we are either naturally selfish, meaning we take. Or we are selfless, meaning we give. While either direction is totally fine, there is a sweet spot right between selfish and selfless that I call the Empowered Self.

Nature's natural rhythm is the balance of giving and receiving. This is where abundance and prosperity consciousness exists, which we will go into later within the book.

We are going to focus on the two extremes of selfishness and selflessness. The taker and the giver both fear that they are not enough, each originating from the inside and looking to find value from external validation.

The taker. It feels excellent to receive. I don't know anyone that doesn't enjoy receiving. However, there is a tipping point between receiving and deviating into a taker. A taker is trying to fill a void within. They are not able to generate sustainable energy from inside themselves, and they need to get it externally.

The giver. It feels good to be of service; however, there is a tipping point, and the giver exhausts their internal resources and becomes void within. They are not able to feel the value of what they are providing and become numb to everything.

I am a natural giver, which means that selfish people are extremely attracted to me. Unless truly respected, this taker/giver connection can quickly turn into a vampire relationship, where the taker fills up their own energy field by consuming the energy of the giver.

I have had many relationships with which I have over given because I wanted to make others feel better, which in turn gave me energy until it didn't. Eventually, I felt taken advantage of and would withdraw my attention from that relationship until the other person recognized they were missing me. I would love to think and feel that they miss me because of who I am as a person. However, I know they often only miss me because

I extend energy that fills them up and makes them feel good, and that is an addictive nectar to a taker.

I also feel that a lot of takers are in denial. They don't recognize their selfishness. Additionally, there are many over givers that do not honor their needs to replenish their extended energy because they do not acknowledge their selflessness.

When we are our Empowered Self, we are right in that sweet spot between selfish and selfless. As individuals, we first get to recognize which side of self we are on. Are you selfish, or are you selfless? With this discovery, we can work on bringing our energetic field back into calibration.

If you are a selfish person, who are you taking from, and how can you give back? This discovery process can be triggering, so be kind to yourself in this unearthing. Do not let yourself get lost in the drama of your selfish behaviors. That isn't what this discovery is meant to do. Often, if a taker is giving, it comes with a condition, meaning they are giving to receive. There is a way to rewire this programming by practicing selfless giving, or unconditional giving. The more you practice just giving because it feels good, the more you will begin to generate your own vital energy, and you will not need to take so much from external relationships. This could be something as simple as over tipping or something as grand as donating every Saturday to a homeless shelter.

If you are a selfless person, who are you over-giving to, and how can you reclaim that energy? I experienced resistance when I started to recognize how much I over gave. I felt selfish, which made me feel extremely uncomfortable because I wasn't fully accepting of my value or my worth. Then I met Orly Alis Steinberg at "The Best Year Ever" event, and she introduced me to the idea of Sacred Selfishness. This concept ultimately reminded me that to be able to give more, I needed first to make sure my cup was full. Having an established self-care or self-love practice is vital for the giver.

For me, this means making sure I honor my needs first thing each day. I spend two hours every morning dedicated to me and making sure I am cared for before I attempt to extend any of my energy externally. I make myself celery juice, lemon water, and coffee. I enjoy contemplative journaling and meditation. I make sure to get my breath active either by exercise or an intentional breathing exercise. Once I am taken care of, I can give without limit, which is a beautiful discovery for me because it makes me feel good to give.

When we balance our selfish and selfless side, we will find Self. A whole self that doesn't need to take beyond what is necessary, and that doesn't need to give beyond what is available. This balance is for the greater good as well, because our energy becomes harmonized.

As we reflect on the greater good, it is important to remember that we are part of it. The more that we can embody this understanding of being part of the greater good, the easier any given situation will be for all.

SELF-AWARE

To be self-aware means that you are aware of your external expression and the internal state of being. This is a conscious connection to your character, values, feelings, motives, and desires, regardless of whether you identify as being "good" or "bad."

Spiritual bypassing, which is a defense mechanism of only looking at the divine alignment to remain in a state of "bliss," has become commonplace for new-age people. This practice disconnects us from our deeper, more complicated feelings. There are a significant amount of people claiming to be "awakened." To a certain degree, perhaps this is true; however, I have found the more "awakened" I become, the less I know, and the more there is to learn. They call it the path to enlightenment for a reason. The journey is never fully completed within our physical form; we choose moment by moment to be "awake" within our awareness.

The discovery of profound inner truth can be a painful process that makes being self-aware a practice for the everyday. This means that if I become out of alignment with my integrity, I call myself out so that I may realign. This also means that when I am in a deep state of awareness, I practice humility so that my ego doesn't jump on stage running amuck with the insight and wisdom I receive.

Societal structures, established during the industrial revolution, were designed to take away from the uniqueness of you. We were put into a funnel and told to go to school, get a job, have a family, retire, and die.

Schools are designed to program compliance in preparation for the workforce. Jobs are created to put people in a box to achieve the bottom line of a corporation's goal.

Institutions are intended to help you see what you can contribute to this socially constructed world that was made up of people who are long since passed. From a young age, our imaginations are squashed, we are told we can't (fill in the blank), we are encouraged to chase careers with higher earning potential, and ideas attached to our creative development are disregarded as childish dreams.

Our uniqueness is lost, as society builds the prison of Modern Fear, discouraging us from being ourselves.

Socialization causes adults to think they are doing what is best for their children by forcing them to fit into the same funnel they moved through. Childhood fantasies are often nudged in the direction of a good education and career, again, the funnel that takes away from the child's unique creative genius and internal power.

We are encouraged to bury our feelings within and to project what society thinks is best.

Lost as an individual, imprisoned in Modern Fear, unsure of your values, thoughts, and beliefs. The need to conform prevents you from expressing your genuine self.

What is not expressed is suppressed, and it will come about again. Suppressed feelings tend to explode in emotional outbursts such as anger, frustration, or stress, which in turn create increased anger, frustration, or stress in life.

The only true way out of Modern Fear is to know yourself through recognition and awareness. You must be willing to accept all of your truths. Forgive yourself for all of your past behaviors, learn from yourself, and forge a new path of sovereignty for liberation and enjoyment.

Deep inner self-work is directly connected to the level you will be able to become self-aware.

Do not be fooled! A life of liberation, a life filled with enjoyment, also requires a willingness to accept limitations that you cannot control. To release and expand your full potential, you must dedicate yourself to finding and exploring the invisible prisons of Modern Fear. **This is a journey of a lifetime and not an instant fix.**

The more self-aware you become, the more clearly you can define your intentions for this exploration for freedom within yourself. Focus your attention on what it is you are manifesting, and strengthen your willpower to raise your vibrational bar, because this journey is not always comfortable, **but** it is always rewarding if you are willing to walk through the valley.

108 | MODERN FEAR: THE INVISIBLE PRISON

To break through the prison of my mind, I harnessed all of my willpower, including my thoughts, feelings, and actions. They all had to align to break through the barriers within myself, which is only possible by practicing self-awareness on all fronts.

Sometimes breaking free of the mind and discovering full self-awareness sucks and feels terrible. I have thought, "Cool, I don't need to do any more work," and felt like giving up. But I knew my soul wanted to know, so I kept going deeper into myself, into and through the pain of the mind, so that on the other side, there is no more suffering.

There is a great power within and all around you. This energy force is the fire of your soul's desire. You deserve more and will be more; however, you must proactively get involved with your evolution to your higher self.

Fear can be your best friend, but it can also be your worst enemy. When you become aware of yourself, all parts of yourself, the good, the bad, and the ugly, fear can no longer be your worst enemy, because there is nothing within you to fear.

By choosing to practice self-awareness, you are also deciding how fear will affect your life.

GET TO KNOW YOUR BAD SELF

I would love to introduce you to Bad Leah. She is the strongest person I know, and she has definitely gone through layers of abuse and down the path of well-being through a healing journey.

Bad Leah came forth as protection because of the painful fear I experienced. I claimed her as my identity during my partying years; however, she has always been part of me.

I admire the strength of Bad Leah and her courage. It is because of her that together we are brave enough to share our most vulnerable stories. In this section, I am going to open up with some vivid feelings and details about my abuse. Please be gentle with yourself if these words are triggering to you. I have been on this intentional inner self-discovery journey for over a decade. I have done deep inner work with people I trust, and I have spent years in contemplation within the peace of my secluded home, feeling safe enough to discover the layers of my most intimate, inner truths.

In my life, I have experienced abuse by multiple people; family, neighbor, mom's partner, boyfriend, and someone that I thought was a friend. I have been molested, raped, mentally, physically, and emotionally abused.

I have been isolated away from anyone who loved me by my abuser, so I could only seek support from the person that destroyed me. Life was hopeless on an endless downward spiral.

I was lost. My soul, that part of me that wanted to live, was buried at a very young age. I always felt like I was acting in life instead of living life. I cursed everything and everyone outside of me. I was not safe, I couldn't protect myself, and I stopped caring. I was bitter, broken, and destructive.

At the age of twelve, I started drinking and smoking cigarettes and weed. By thirteen, I introduced LSD and mushrooms. By fourteen, I was using hard drugs such as meth and cocaine, and by fifteen, I was sexually active. I was running with the wrong crowd and believed I was so fucking cool. I was arrested and convicted for forgery, theft, and obstruction of

110 | MODERN FEAR: THE INVISIBLE PRISON

justice, and was put on probation.

I wanted to shut off the angry voices inside my head, so I numbed all my feelings, to the point that pain became the norm in my mental, emotional, and physical suffering. I was trying to convince myself that I didn't care. I didn't think that my life was of value and often contemplated suicide, considering how much easier life would be if I were dead.

However, I was born with a warrior fighter in me. I know that this warrior energy is my absolute faith in myself; however, to Bad Leah, the warrior energy was pure resiliency. The woman who is typing these words right now is the embodied warrior fighter. However, I was buried deep within Bad Leah, a dim energetic force that had forgotten how to feel due to the trauma and drama that I was experiencing and creating. The embodied warrior force is the part of me that I feel is connected to being a lightworker.

Even though I was doing my best to destroy myself with my behavioral choices, there was something within me, calling me towards something better, a way out of the hell that I was imprisoned within. I hoped for a future where I was safe, secure, and stable. I wanted independence from the life that my mother had created. In an egocentric way at that point in time, I thought I was better than my current social status, and I wanted to prove I could not be crushed, hope fueled with anger drove my persevering energy.

At sixteen, I moved out of my mother's trailer, located in a meth infested trailer park behind a seedy hotel, and moved in with my boyfriend at the time. I thought that I was making the right move for myself by getting away from my mother. At the time, I still blamed her for all of the wrongs in my life. I couldn't have been more wrong. He slowly isolated me from all of my friends and spoke to me in demeaning ways. He stalked me to ensure I was going where I said I would. He made me believe I was nothing without him. He was a taker and sucked everything out of me, and at the time, I was willing to give it to him because I wanted so desperately to be needed.

Even still, through all of the hardship of my youth, I maintained an exceptionally high GPA in school. I worked full time at a grocery store, and I graduated a year early from high school.

A couple of years into this abusive relationship, my boyfriend came home one day and shared that he hadn't been working for the past month and had no money to pay for rent. All of my safety, security, and stability were yanked right out from underneath me. There was an explosion within our home. I will never forget the anger in his eyes, his fist flying at my face, and the absolute terror that held me, prisoner, in shock. Just before impact, he changed course and hit the wall. My body went from complete fear to instant relief as I recognized that the outcome could have been significantly worse than a hole in the wall.

"Never again," came a whisper from inside of me. This was the first time that I had ever heard my intuition, and with it, a dim fire sparked. I knew I had to do something to protect myself.

I was destroyed, I couldn't feel anything anymore, numb and devoid of life, there was nothing left of me. I was a shell of a woman and completely hopeless. Where was I to go?

I have had many guardian angels come into my life, and during this period, my friend's mom, Kate, took me in. She provided me a loving home with an abundance of food and safety. I will never forget Kate's generosity. She saved my life during my darkest time by giving me space to figure out what was next.

Once outside of the abusive situation, I got excessively angry. Mostly at myself; thus, my inner abuse cycle began. My boyfriend was no longer there to abuse me, so I took that on myself. When this anger wasn't destroying me on the inside, it provided another powerful force driving me and directing me forward one step at a time. I knew that I never wanted to go back to where I was before.

I applied to community college and was accepted into a laboratory technician program and started to focus on my education and my future. Even though I was looking to improve my situation, I was continuing to party, excessively drinking, and staying out late.

Bad Leah was born during this moment in my life, and she harnessed the power of the mother fucker. I know that this statement can be offensive to some, and for that, there is nothing I can do. The power of the mother fucker was my mantra, my affirmation, my guiding light as I fought tooth and nail to better my life. I was angry, and I wanted to prove to the world that I was more than a poor, abused woman.

The power of the mother fucker is the inner part of myself that is my junkyard dog. I will protect myself. I will stand up for myself. I will not cower, and I will not waiver. This part of myself was my best friend, guardian, and protector for many years. Until eventually, it became my enemy and started to cause damage to those who loved me. I had closed off my compassion and had become overly reactive.

Bad Leah is self-absorbed. She lives for the thrills, loves to party, and seeks immediate self-rewards. She takes what she wants when she wants, how she wants. Honestly, she is so much fun there isn't an adventure she would miss. And yet, she can be a total bitch; she is selfish and doesn't empathetically care about anything because she was numb to unconditional love.

I believe that I am a soul experiencing a human life, and Bad Leah is my human side that I get to spend my entire life embodied within. I, Bad Leah, have caused wave after wave of heartaches. I, Bad Leah, have let loose and gone down so many unpredictable paths. I, Bad Leah, have abused my mind, body, and soul. I, Bad Leah, have lived in the invisible prison of Modern Fear.

Bad Leah is still with me. She is my shadow side and life partner. I know this because she and I have gone through enough healing together that I no longer need to fear the damage she can cause. Instead, I now relish in her spirit for celebrating the present moment. Bad Leah doesn't live imprisoned within my chaotic mind prisons anymore. She now walks within me, residing in my heart, and I truly love her.

Do you have a Bad Self that creates a little too much drama in your life? How can you create a new storyline for your Bad Self, so you can release the guilt, shame, and anger that comes with being human?

SECTION 2

RECLAIM

---

*Retrieve or recover (something previously lost,
given, or paid); obtain the return of.*

*"People suffer because they are caught in their views.
As soon as we release those views, we are free,
and we don't suffer anymore."*
Thich Nhat Hanh

We are encouraged to "let go" and "release" negative things like situations, memories, or feelings. These "negative" things are energy leaks that cause dis-ease. Our mind, body, and spirit will become weighed down if we choose to continue to carry around this dis-ease with us.

As we learn to release, it is essential to remember that we are meant to be whole beings. If you are letting one thing go, make sure to choose what you are reclaiming so that the old energy does not reappear. We are habituated beings. Old patterns will remain present until new ones form. Whatever you let go of, you will receive back, unless you reclaim different energy in its place.

Be consciously aware of what you are reclaiming, such as time, relationship, or influence over your feelings.

PRESENT LIFESTYLE–RECLAIM YOUR TIME

Your current lifestyle is how you allocate your time and what you do with the present and proximate moments.

- What are your primary commitments to your current lifestyle?
- Are you a workaholic?
- Do you put your family's needs first?
- How many hours do you spend disconnected from your external reality, in front of your television, on the computer, or in front of your devices?
- Do you seek decompression through the use of mind-altering substances?
- Is there always something that needs to be done?
- Where does your health and wellness fit come into your lifestyle?
- What is your commitment to you?

I often refer to myself as a recovering people pleaser. My own Modern Fear, not being able to feel my feelings, blinded me to the fact that I used to put my own needs secondary to others.

In truth, I craved acceptance from anyone that would give it to me. I wanted to feel significant to others, so I busted my butt in my education, career, and relationships to feel worthy. However, when I got home, I was exhausted because I was always overextending my energy.

There were many weeks after working my full-time day job and a side hustle bartending, that by the time Sunday came around, I would lock myself away in my bedroom and disappear, as I tried to "catch-up" on a lack of sleep. In attempting to recharge, I would find myself feeling depressed and lonely because I had overextended all of my inner source energy. If my schedule wasn't packed with taking care of extra things, I would become very uncomfortable because my mind would start a "lazy" narrative, causing me to feel guilt and shame. I didn't like being alone with my thoughts and feelings. In truth, I didn't like myself. I was angry at the pain of my traumas and the pain I caused others. I felt like a failure in life because I had set an unattainable bar for myself, trying to prove my value. I didn't value myself because my worth was buried.

Let me paint a picture of the average day of how I used to live life and see if you can relate.

- 5 a.m. – I am a practitioner of The Miracle Morning, so I would spend the first hour of my day focused on Leah, journaling, reading, affirmations, meditation, and drinking my coffee nice and slow.
- 6 a.m. – I would begin to get ready for a day in corporate America, quick shower, throw on clothes, and rush out the door
- 7 a.m. – Off to the park and ride, to be packed into an overly crowded bus, just to stall all forward momentum in a traffic-jammed expressway for a ridiculous amount of time.
- 8 a.m. – Office arrival, stop by the coffee shop, grab my Americano, and quiche for breakfast.
- 8:30 a.m. – Arrive at my desk, turn on my computer and sit there for hours, typing and clicking the mouse.
- Noon – My favorite time of day, I would rush down to my CrossFit class, and I would WORK my body, pushing it to go beyond the limits of the day before.
- 1 p.m. – Back at my desk with something quick to eat, so that I could sit there again, typing and clicking the mouse.
- 4 p.m. – Squeeze myself back onto the jam-packed bus.
- 5 p.m. – Back home, I quickly changed into my bartending clothes and was out the door for my shift.
- 6 p.m. to 11 p.m. - I worked behind the bar at Neptune Theater, listening to amazing shows and serving a multitude of patrons.
- Midnight – Back home and into bed, just to hear the alarm at 5 a.m.

I lived within this unsustainable energetic level for years because I had programmed myself to be a constant doer trying to prove my value to myself. My morning practice was providing minimal support; however, I was so drained that it was insufficient to refill my cup. It was more like putting a dollar of gas in an empty gas tank. It only took me so far, and then the stress would take over again. I was living a life that was completely driven by paying the bills and just getting by. There wasn't a lot of pleasure. There wasn't a lot of freedom and there definitely was not a high priority on quality by spending nourishing time with people that I loved or loved me.

It had never dawned on me to consider the quality of life I wanted to live until the heartbreak of death entered my reality. Cancer. What a commercialized disease that plagues our culture. The cure, worse than death.

On a rainy Sunday afternoon, my dear friend, Jim, sat across from me in one of our favorite burger restaurants, Two Bells. I could tell that something was weighing heavily on him. As he spoke, it was hard for him to maintain direct eye contact. "It is a very rare form of cancer. There is not a lot of research on this type yet. The doctors are saying the worst-case scenario is under a year, and the best case might be up to six years." I instantly felt within my intuition that we were looking at the shorter time frame. My gift of knowing at times feels like a curse.

Tears welled in my eyes, and my mind raced. What do I say to this news? "Oh, Jim." It came out as a whisper. I so loved this man and his wife. They had adopted me figuratively in my thirties and were my soul parents and dear friends.

"What can I do?" I asked.

"Just be you," he replied.

That was all he needed to say. At that moment, I put on my familiar warrior armor. I knew death. In this time of transition for Jim, I harnessed all of my strength to be there for Jim and his family, adding this desired responsibility to my already packed life. I knew where this was headed, and I did not want to hide from my sadness, knowing his death was on the horizon. I didn't want to run away from the potential pain of my broken heart. How do I even begin to say good-bye? I didn't, I leaned in, I held steady, and I made sure to be part of the last months of my dear friend's life in every possible way. I reclaimed my time from all the meaningless distractions and focused my energy on being present to the unavoidable truth that Jim's precious time was running out. Jim was going to die, and he so desperately wanted to live. Jim's essence embodied the passion of life.

Jim was a distinguished gentleman. He was kind. He was a storyteller, and he was one hell of a host; dinner parties around his dining room table, with candles lit, wine overflowing, delectable dinners, decadent desserts, and endless conversations. These are moments that I will treasure forever. I can still hear his laugh. I can even see his body shake as the joy moved through him. Jim's charisma for life inspired hope for me about the style of my future. I hope to replicate the hospitality that Jim and Mel provided for the rest of my life. I knew by witnessing Jim and his wife's way of life that I wanted to be surrounded by people I loved and who loved me in return.

When cancer moved to his brain, I knew it was time to say good-bye before it was too late. I stopped by the house to see if Mel needed anything. We sat in the kitchen speaking quietly, Jim in the other room resting, watching television.

I went into the den and sat next to him as he reached for the remote control to turn down the T.V. Jim had become a shell of the man he once was. The "treatment" had prevented his stomach from being able to hold down any nutrients and had robbed his taste buds of any pleasure.

Jim was never one to express too many emotions, but it didn't matter. I knew the way he felt about me. As I sat next to him, inside, I braced myself, which encouraged me to stay strong. "I love you, Jim. I wanted to make sure to tell you today."

"Oh my, Leah!" his hand reaching for his heart, "I love you too."

"You have inspired me to live, Jim. You are always going to be with me. Thank you for being in my life."

I leaned over and gave Jim the last hug I would ever give him. It was an awkward side hug, definitely not my best. I was in a hurry to get out because inside, I was losing it, my composure cracking. I stopped at the doorway of the kitchen and turned back to find Jim sitting there with his hands held as if they were still holding mine. I didn't go back to him, and to this day, this memory lingers with me. Why didn't I go back for one last embrace, one last moment? Why? Modern Fear is why; I was afraid of my feelings, and I was bolting.

The next time I saw Jim, he was still conscious and able to sit upright, but the Jim I loved was gone. His physical body was holding on, and yet his mind was hurriedly fading. Jim had one of the sharpest minds, to witness this dissolving broke my heart.

Jim quickly went on hospice. The last night of his life, I was at his home, sitting on the back porch with his daughter, while his wife and sister were inside with him. When we came back inside, and I was preparing to leave, Mel came rushing down the stairs, "Jim is dying." I could feel it. She was right.

I decided to leave. I felt that at this point, it was a family affair. As I shut the door to his house, the click was deafening. I rested my hand on the front door, perhaps supporting myself and also sending love to my passing friend, "Good-bye Jim, I love you."

I walked away. I sat in my car, stunned, speechless, tearless, and devoid of a response. What was I doing with my life? It was all I could consider at that moment. I returned home, and an hour later, I received the news that Jim had passed. What a light our world lost that day.

The following days were spent drifting through required responsibilities and quality time with my boyfriend in his art room, aka "the dungeon." We sat there dreaming together about a slower pace of life in our Montana rental home that we owned up Rock Creek, just outside of Missoula. We dreamed of the self-sustaining life that we wanted to create, growing our food, raising our meat, the solar power we would use, on and on this dream saturated my current reality.

The dungeon was a fantastic room, shag carpet, wood-paneled walls, and brimming with Nick's creative energy. I sat on the couch with our boxer, Scrappy, snuggled up to me, and we were lost in the thought of a simplified Montana life. I looked at Nick and said, "If you told me you would want to move back to Montana, I would tell you let's do it."

Nick simply replied, "I want to move to Montana," and the trajectory of our life was forever changed.

Jim passed away on February 27th. On March 1st, the decision to move back to Montana was made, and on May 1st, we pulled into the driveway of our new life in Rock Creek.

When you take the time to listen to what your soul is indeed calling you to do, there is no denying that the Universe will open up a path for you to find your way.

Reality set in. The 180-degree shift in the way I spent time smacked me a few times and then backhanded me some more. I struggled. I had NO idea what to do with all of my time. The external obligations dissolved when I disappeared into the woods. It was time for me to go deep within myself.

I made the conscious choice to live my life less packed with activities and more focused on stillness. I moved through life in calm silence, witnessing the surfacing of buried memories, moving through forgotten or blocked suffering. I recharged myself in the slowness so that I could reclaim all of my lost and overextended energies.

You see, the life that I had designed up until moving back to Montana was about "making it" in the rat-race. It was about rising to the top, proving to the world and myself that I mattered. I was seeking external validation and needed others to see I was significant and that I did have value. I had designed a life that lacked my soul's style. In the solitude of the Sapphire Mountains, waking with the rising sun and slowing with the settling of dusk, I got to know myself on an incredibly intimate level. The excavation/reflection process was brutal. I had buried, forgotten, and lied to myself about so many things. **When there are no external distractions, there is no place to hide from yourself,** and my choice to move and shift my lifestyle was the catalyst I needed to face my truth.

SOCIAL LIFESTYLE

There is no right or wrong when it comes to how you choose to spend your free time. You were born human with the gift of free will. Your social time is the opportunity to do whatever it is you want; however, social behaviors do affect the quality of your life. This section is an invitation to move from a lifestyle of distraction to a lifestyle of intention.

Drugs or alcohol, meditation or workouts, food, or sugar all alter the chemical composition of your body, your mind, and, consequently, your feelings. They either stimulate you to feel better or worse.

Are you conscious of the effects your social lifestyle has on you?

Are you seeking an escape or a release from your situational realities?

I started abusing substances at the age of twelve. Due to my traumatic experiences, intoxication was a perfect habit to suppress my feelings and memories that I couldn't understand or knew how to handle.

I felt freer under the influence, but there was always a tipping point during my intoxication, where I was guaranteed to become sad, then angry. The fury that was buried inside of me would explode. I lashed out the worst at those who I knew loved me most, the ones I knew would still be there for me, even though I did awful and hurtful things.

Honestly, in my own experience, it wasn't the intoxication that caused the most damage; it was the abusive self-talk that followed the next day, along with the hangover. I was disappointed in myself, questioning what I had said or done. I was so afraid of facing the life that I had experienced that it was preventing me from being present in the life I was living.

At this point in my life, I have done enough inner self-work with my shadow side that I do not desire the escape of intoxication. It has lost its value for me. I am not saying that there is anything wrong with the use of substances; I believe and know they have their place and purpose. What I am saying is the use of substances without conscious recognition is a highway to the danger zone of Modern Fear. For me, it was alcohol, the one substance that is legal and easily accessible to anyone, and yet destroys so many lives.

If you are imprisoned by Modern Fear, you are more likely to have behavioral tendencies that are focused on escape, such as intoxication, avoidance, or procrastination.

What are you avoiding?

Are your social behaviors aiding your personal development and the greater good? If the answer to this question is no, then it is time to take an intimate look in the mirror and consider some new hobbies or activities. Owning responsibility for hard truths is one of the most effective ways to reclaim your energy from unsupportive behaviors.

To socially change, you might have to consider what you do for fun and whom you are associating with while having fun. People that are toxic for your growth will not want you to change. Be aware of these toxic people as they come forward during your evolution and your liberation from Modern Fear.

THE INFLUENCE OF YOUR ENVIRONMENT

Within this section, we will explore the environment of your body, home, local community, and the world. What is your current relationship and awareness of your environment?

Every single action you take or do not take has an impact on your environment. Believe it or not, accept this or don't, you impact everything. The world feels you. I feel you. Can you feel yourself?

The human body, our immediate environment, is a sacred temple that many of us take for granted. Before going any further, I want to point out how freaking cool the human body is. The mass of our existence, the flesh, bones, muscles, fibers, fluids, and whatever else I am not listing, is a collective agreement of trillions of cells working together to give you a vessel to experience this world in which we live.

Talk about witnessing a community coming together and creating something extraordinary, YOU.

Culturally, appreciation for this wholeness has been diluted because our society is obsessed with the body and how it looks. It is incredibly easy to hide our internal suffering by creating an immaculate appearance, with the right clothes, hair done up, and face put on. When if we were more considerate of how our body feels rather than looks, we might make several different choices in life, like not following the next diet fad, or resting when we are tired rather than pushing ourselves to exhaustion.

Life happens in motion. Honoring this principle with your body is hard work. Movement of our body is typically one of the last priorities on our to-do list. The simple fact is if you do not practice movement, your life will be robbed of mobility. I know this personally, as I sit a lot for my job, and every time I stand up after sitting for long periods, it takes a minute for my hips to get under me so that I can walk normally. In trying to support my hips, I purchased a standing desk, which absolutely helps but only if I stand at it. More often than not, I am sitting because that is my habituated practice. Changing long life behaviors takes time.

I fell in love with working out in my mid-twenties while taking a body pump class. Beverly, the instructor, made movement fun, and she also introduced me to the idea of gratitude for my mobility. Every time my body would be screaming just to stop, I would hear Beverly's voice over the microphone, "Be grateful you are able." This simple statement resonated so deeply because I am grateful, and with this gratitude, I could push through.

I have not always honored the physical demands of my body. My mind would push my body's limits, often leading to injury; where I thought I was doing well for my body, I was causing it harm. If you want to push your body, that's cool. Just remember it's what is holding you together, so kindness matters. If you rip your muscles apart with an intense workout, make sure to nurture them with good nutrition and perhaps an Epsom salt soak. Remember that recovery is part of the movement. Make sure you get proper rest, allowing your body time to rejuvenate.

Walking most days for 30 minutes is a simple practice in honoring your body. This practice gets you outside for fresh air and mobility. Walking is also a great time to contemplate something that needs a little more attention. Even if your job has you on your feet all day, you should still be walking for 30 minutes. Get outside, explore, move your body.

I would also invite you to challenge your body with different types of movement, whatever sounds fun. I have been a rock climber, an aerialist, a scuba instructor, and have tried all kinds of dance; one of my recent favorites is hula-hooping, thanks to my dear friend Jessica, the founder of Hula Healing. Check out her website https://www.hulahealer.com/ if you are interested in more play!

Approximately 50% of your body is water. It has its cycle where it will evaporate or be excreted, so you must replenish the water in your body. The most important thing you can drink is water. When I first wake up, I down a glass of water before I put anything else in my body. I started this powerful daily practice years ago, and it increased my energy once it became an established habit in my routine.

The greatest thing you can ever do for your body is to review the way you eat. My relationship with life changed when my relationship with food evolved.

I grew up eating cheap, highly processed food. I was a fast-food junkie until my thirties, and for a period in my early twenties, I lived off of Coke-Cola and Ding Dongs. Never once in all my years did I ever imagine I was causing my body harm. Our grocery stores and restaurants are filled with foods that cause physical disease. There seems to be no accountability of these companies that produce or provide these types of "food" and the destruction they cause to our health.

I was introduced to the idea of whole foods, meaning eating only items that come from nature. If an item of food wasn't around a hundred years ago, maybe we shouldn't eat it. I started reading labels, and my life changed. I was shocked at the number of ingredients that I couldn't identify. If I couldn't pronounce the ingredients, I would question, is this really food? I am now a person who refuses to eat chemicals. If I can't pronounce the ingredient, I don't eat it. I want to eat food, not chemicals. When I made this transition, a veil was lifted. Mentally, the fog cleared, physically, inflammation, and random pains disappeared, and emotionally, I became less erratic. These personal results confirmed that the "food" I had been eating was harming me.

The body is a machine that will only perform as well as the fuel that is put into it. The quality of your nourishment will either hinder or enhance your lifestyle. If you are eating primarily fast food, you are hurting yourself. If you are eating processed foods, you are hurting yourself. If you are eating food filled with chemicals, antibiotics, and hormones, you are hurting yourself. If you do not believe me, I challenge you to eliminate these foods from your diet for 28 days and see how you feel. Commit fully, no cheating, and be honest. I promise that you will experience results.

I know my food beliefs are extreme. That is because I understand that food is our first medicine. The quality of the food's life cycle determines the quality of energy that it provides to you as you eat it. I purchase my meat from a single source, meaning I buy a quarter of a cow and half a pig every year, and that is the meat we eat (although occasionally a quality sourced chicken or turkey will end up on the plate). We purchase the majority of vegetables from local farmers and also grow our own. The bread we eat comes from a local baker. Yes, of course, I still eat pre-made food. However, I tried to buy from companies that are aligned with the greater good. I consider the sourcing of their ingredients. Food is a lifestyle for me, and it is where I spend the majority of my money because everything about it makes me feel good.

I would like to share with you that I don't hold myself, prisoner to rigorous rules when it comes to food. I try to live within an 80/20 rule or 90/10 rule. Meaning that the majority of the time, I live within the boundaries of the food morality I have created. I also honor the fact that not everyone lives within my boundaries, so I give myself some flexibility. If I go to someone's home and they have cooked me dinner and don't know about chemicals and food, I will gladly eat and partake in the loving energy they have extended in preparing the meal. If I want to eat a huge piece of German chocolate cake from the country restaurant down the road, I will. Rather than punishing myself mentally or getting stressed out in fear or judgment, I simply connect to the food, give it appreciation for the joy it brings me and ask my body to allow whatever goodness of the food to be absorbed and the rest to be excreted.

Moving from the body, we next get to explore your home, which is your immediate, external environment. It is the one space you have total control over. Material things have energetic weight to them. When we are trapped in Modern Fear, and we are not connected to our feelings, it is a common practice to try to buy things to make us feel better. As a result, our home becomes cluttered with meaningless items that have no value or lasting joy except instant gratification.

If you find yourself cluttered and burdened on the inside, take a moment to look around your home and see if it is cluttered with items that do not serve you. Living within clutter is a chaotic experience. We can become blind to the fact that our home is even cluttered because it makes us feel uncomfortable to see how much stuff we have accumulated. And for what?

Do you know what is in your house? If not, it is a great time to reclaim your space for what you want it to be and not just a circumstance of mindless accumulation.

I am not a person that is attached to material things because I never had them. Growing up, I dreamt of having nice things. However, it is not my driving force. The practice of decluttering my space is something I truly enjoy. To organize and declutter is a contemplative practice that allows for an in-depth internal evaluation of how each item is impacting your life. Essential versus non-essential. I love this tool of picking up an item and asking if it is essential in my life, and if the answer is "no," I like to get rid of it. I know another tool that Marie Kondo uses is asking, "Does this (fill in the blank) bring me joy," if the answer is "no," thank it and release it.

If your home is immaculate, and yet your closets are packed to the brim, what is that really saying? Again, an immaculate presentation can often mean something uncomfortable may be buried within. Items behind closed doors matter. All that stuff is still occupying the space of your precious home.

Our habits within our home represent our habits outside of the house. If you conserve within your home, you are likely to care about conservation outside of your home. If you recycle within your home, then you are going to look to purchase from businesses that care about recycling. If you are active within your home, then you will be active outside of your home. Our habits of actions originate within our homes.

Locally, the community in which we live determines what is available to us. Inner-city, low-income people, do not have the same access as suburban dwellers. There are plenty of people who have never seen a real strawberry and don't know that the strawberry jelly within their Pop Tart at one time was a real fruit.

The mainstream, modern relationship with our environment has caused a disconnection of knowing the source from where the items we purchase come. Does the majority of your shopping take place in large box stores, giving your money to major conglomerates? Most of these entities only care about their profit margins and not necessarily about their impact on the environment or you as a human.

Are you doing your part within your local community to evaluate the responsibility of your impact? Do you have a "recycle" bin that you put your recyclables in without really putting in the appropriate effort to make sure the items can be recycled? The majority of what you think is being "recycled" is finding its way to the landfill because we culturally put in a half-assed effort to ensure items can actually be recycled.

Do you ever go to your farmer's market and buy produce fresh off the vine, from the person who grew it? Have you ever met the rancher who raises the meat that you eat? Do you support local small businesses so that your direct community can thrive? How connected are you to your local environment?

If you are a consumer that chooses to give your hard-earned money over to major conglomerates, you have an opportunity to reconnect to your local environment and economy. These major entities see no value in who you are as a person. They sell you products that will poison your home, your body, and our land. They take. These types of industries are significant influencers for Modern Fear because they don't care about how you feel or your well-being, and manipulate you through marketing. In spending your dollars with these types of companies, you are giving your energy over to an entity that is not energetically giving back to you.

I love walking into a local, small business to do my shopping because I know when I spend my money there, my purchase is a blessing, and there is an immediate impact of my dollar. Have you ever reflected on the values associated with how the products you purchased are sourced? It is our responsibility to our local community to impact as many immediate lives as possible through the power of our purchasing.

Everything we do with our body, our home, and our local environment affects our global impact. We are not separate from Earth. We are part of Earth. I feel that it is important that I disclose that I do love our planet, the home we all share. I know that I am a product of her creation and I feel incredibly blessed to be in her existence. I also know that Earth is the most potent living entity I have personally ever witnessed. Our planet is badass, and this should matter to you because you are one of its creations, absolutely everything is! Just like all life, Earth has had its own cycles of birth and death. It has gone through five different mass extinctions. Humans are rapidly causing her to be destroyed, yet I am not worried about her. Earth knows how to recover. Species become extinct, not planets (unless the sun burns them up).

Our global lack of awareness is a human problem, not an Earth problem.

If you believe in karma, meaning what goes around comes around, how you treat our Mother Earth should be in your regular consideration. The environment is a reflection of how humans are treating themselves.

Nature is one of our greatest teachers, and yet the drive to be successful within an urban landscape can separate us from this knowing. It is time to remember this unified connection. When was the last time you contemplated and celebrated your harmony with nature or accepted responsibility for the harm you cause to nature? When was the last time you planted your feet in her grass? When was the last time you stopped to feel the wisdom of a giant tree trunk? When was the last time you bathed in her waters? When was the last time you witnessed and honored all the other living beings with whom we share this sacred planet?

If you have not gotten lost in her beauty recently, then my friend, I invite you to go on an adventure. Find a park, a beach, a river, or stream and sit down, close your eyes, and witness the power that is always available to your senses. You are one of Earth's creations, bond with your Mother. This invitation is for you to recognize that you are not separate from nature; you just might not yet have a bonded relationship with nature. It takes a dedicated presence to sink in and slow down to nature's vibration.

Earth is a vast place. Most of us never leave the region in which we are born. In my world travels, I have witnessed cultures that still live off the land and cultures that no longer know the land is there. Our life perspective is connected to our experiences, so if you have never experienced an environment outside of your local community, the perspective in which you see the world is through that limited lens.

Each one of us is responsible for ensuring that we are living within a safe, stable, and secure environment. This physical and spatial awareness is key in reclaiming our ability to feel the full spectrum of our feelings and release ourselves from Modern Fear.

THE MEANING OF TRUTH IS RELATIVE

Beyond you or me is a force that holds us all together. This bonding force is a great mystery, and yet it connects each and every one of us. I believe that there is no separation between anything, we are fully connected, and we are either living in harmony with that connection or disharmony through resistance. It is my life's practice to bring myself into harmonious alignment with the greater good, which means that I don't always get my way. Sometimes what is best for me doesn't serve anyone else, so I practice the uncomfortable feeling of compromising; knowing what is best for me isn't what is needed.

I have my truth, you have your truth, and together we have our collective truth. What we feel is true to ourselves creates the foundation for our beliefs. Scientifically it is proven the average temperature of the Earth is rising, and yet there are still people that do not believe in global warming. Young Earth Creationism is a religious belief that God created lifeforms 10,000 years ago, and this truth doesn't work for me because I believe the dinosaur fossils are real. **The practice here is allowing different truths to exist without taking it personally.**

As a culture, we are quick to shame or shun others when their truths do not align with ours. It creates conflict and requires that we practice conscious listening skills to allow for multiple meanings of truth to co-exist. Imagine if we all allowed for each other's belief structure, as long it was not harmful to others, to exist without persecution. I grew up in the Mormon religion, and as such, I was baptized Mormon. Although this religion has never been my adult belief, I had a Catholic friend tell me I was condemned to hell because of a decision that was made for me when I was eight years old. Their truth didn't feel good, and yet, I allowed for the perspective without taking it personally.

Honesty is the ability to be vulnerable to our truth. Confusion and dis-ease happen when we do not allow the appropriate amount of space for relative truth to exist. My belief does not have to be your belief, just as I do not have to believe as you do. In this situation, the meaning behind our individual truths becomes relative to our personal experiences. In the course of conversation with a friend, I discovered that they didn't believe in global warming, and my gut reaction was disbelief. However, it is not my responsibility to tell someone else how they should think, and at that moment, rather than trying to convince them that global warming was real, we simply agreed to disagree, and that was beautiful. It is my responsibility to be a kind and compassionate human and not to shame others if their truths do not have the same meaning as mine.

In life, we are expressing truth from our personal lens. Those who are in alignment with our beliefs will be attracted to our truths, and a collective truth grows strength. Because of this, it is imperative to have a confident understanding of how you perceive the world. Know how your beliefs influence the meaning of your truths and how your leadership is going to inspire others. Contemplation is a perfect practice when exploring your truths and their origin. Where do you find yourself holding to a belief without wavering? Does that serve your greater good, or is it something that is holding you back?

Not everyone is going to agree with you all the time (this is a good thing). The trick is to not be in a place of judgment when we are in a state of disbelief. We can reclaim that energy by practicing respect for another person's journey by being a witness to their perspective, without the desire to control their beliefs. Have an open mind and heart so that both truths can grow roots together.

FAITH

Science and logic theorize and test facts that confirm matter was created out of many explosions, originating with the Big Bang. Faith and belief allow for the imagination of consciousness to dance, play, and create our experience called Reality.

There are plenty of people out there who believe God created the world, and perhaps that could be true. I know that it is important for me not to be too rigid when I don't have a full understanding of a belief. I, too, believe in a higher power, which I refer to as Source, also known as God. I have an intimate relationship with Source because I know and understand that the higher power is not separate from me, and in fact, it resides within me, just as it does within you.

I wonder regularly, when did the belief of God originate? More importantly, when was the power of God taken out of us and given away to the invisible force of fear? I imagine at the beginning of human evolution, God was more of an intuitive knowing or a feeling from within. Then there was a shift in perspective, and God became external, anchored in some sort of absolute which was used to explain the unexplainable, supporting miraculous experiences. Additionally, the weaponized belief of God puts the fear of morality into humans.

Thus the power of faith was born, an invisible force that can only be sensed or experienced first-hand.

Our human experience is a mixture of our physical experience, beliefs, and faith. They ebb and flow with the tides of our life. When something is impossible to believe, we can reclaim that belief by leaning into our faith; our intuition and our heart will show us the way. **When our faith seems lost, it is only buried,** and the belief of its existence is the seed that will offer rebirth.

In my life journey, it was the faith in myself that kept me going. When others didn't believe in me, when my probation officer told me society doesn't want me to succeed when the odds were stacked against me, I

LEAH LOVELIGHT MICHAEL | 133

surrendered to my faith that my life was not forsaken, and it indeed had meaning and purpose.

One thing is for certain; there are great forces at work. To know this, you simply need to spend time connected with nature, explore the badass discoveries of science, or sit in a church and feel the energy of unified connection through faith and shared belief.

RELATIONSHIPS

A relationship is an energetic exchange of time, feelings, and commitment. The most important and often overlooked relationship is the relationship we have with ourselves. Humans are a herd species. It is natural for us to want to be in a relationship with others; however, those external relationships should not take priority over having a relationship of well-being with yourself.

When a person is caught in Modern Fear, their energetic field is in disharmony, and they will have a decreased capacity for empathy, ultimately preventing them from being able to have a deeply connected relationship with others. They are lost in their own world. They are held prisoner by the urge to fighting or fleeing from themselves. It is hard to like ourselves when we cannot feel our gifts. Once you are aware of the presence of Modern Fear in others, you will see it in the relationship you have with yourself; we are all a reflection.

People in your life are there for a reason. At some point, they brought something of significance to the experience in which you want to live. Just like in the decluttering of your home, we need to declutter our relationships. Every connection is an energetic bond. If a relationship is not supporting your greater good, it is essential to let that relationship go. This energetic release gives space to reclaim your energy, which can then be directed towards new relationships aligned to who you are no.

Be honest with yourself and decide if you still want to be in a relationship with that person. That answer is pretty black and white, and yes, you have a choice for all of your relationships. Some relationships require obligation, but once that obligation is complete, so too can the relationship be.

I am not suggesting you leave your relationships, especially if you are invested in them. Instead, this perspective is an invitation to invest your energy differently. Relationships require honesty if they are going to work for the benefit of all parties. Clear communication is the only way to release yourself from Modern Fear when it comes to relationships. Be brave and share your feelings. Non-essential relationships that are dysfunctional will slowly drift apart. Blaming one another for the damage due to the dysfunction will not help the situation.

Blame is a judgmental tendency of its own. You can blame the other person, but then you are not taking responsibility for your contribution to the failing relationship. You can blame yourself, but then you are not considering the other person's responsibility.

Blame only leads to shame.

Observation, consciously acknowledging the need for change, and clear communication is the only things that are going to allow you to transform your relationship. Know what you want to accomplish in each of your relationships and then put forward the action to create this reality. Any other behavior might allow the harmful effects to continue to perpetuate.

Reclaim the knowing that you deserve to be loved and respected by all of your relationships. Release attachment to any relationship that is depleting your energy. Call in regenerative relationships that will support you on your path.

RECLAIMING OLD STORIES

We have already explored how our old stories can hold us prisoner within the identification of a victim. The identity of a victim is one of the most draining energies we can experience, no matter the victimhood.

You do not have to experience painful suffering if you allow for compassion to come through. The character you identify within your past will affect who you are today. Recognize when you are reassuming the identity of a victim, and reclaim your energy from these past transgressions.

Memories can be experienced from two perspectives: as a **participant** or as a **witness**, shifting your participation is a tool to reclaim your old story.

Participant: your thoughts, feelings, and body are bound to this memory; as it surfaces, so do the past emotions that went with it.

There is great healing that can happen by visiting your past from the inside out. Your physical body keeps records of events in your life and will store those events as symptoms of pain or sensation. I love craniosacral therapy for listening to the body. I saw a practitioner to address some soreness in my shoulder, and while her hands held my shoulder, a memory of me as a little girl swinging surfaced. Then my mom came forth in the memory, and I experienced my mom's joy while watching me. Suddenly the pain in my shoulder was released. Energetically, I was out of alignment. I had spent so many years angry and blaming my mother for my suffering. I had forgotten that she was so much fun, too. My pain was holding her love prisoner within my body. When it was released, so did some of the anger I felt.

Physical symptoms are messengers of the past that, if released correctly, can cause you to have visceral releases, which is a deep inward healing response to the feelings of a memory that once caused dis-ease.

Witness: you observe your past as a third party. The person you are today can give love, compassion, and acceptance to the person you were then. There is no judgment for those experiences. For me to be released from Modern Fear, I had to release my inner little girl from my own projected judgment of my origin. I accepted the fact that this part of my story could not be changed, and I was able to hold her with healing compassion.

To love and accept the person you were in your memories creates the ability to love the person you are today.

Until you figure out this road map for participant versus witness, life will be hard at times. If you do not accept a part of yourself from your past, you cannot accept the person you are today, which causes fear in your future. Relieving or wanting to redo your past wastes your energy and gives your power away. Reclaim that power through acceptance, compassion, and forgiveness.

COMPROMISE

We are all part of an existence that is bigger than merely our own individual realities. We are all part of a home, a community, a society, and a planet as a whole. The greater good encompasses all aspects of our existence in the physical reality and the invisible energetic fields. For all of these different parts to flow together in fluid harmony, it is essential to accept the responsibility that we are each part of this greater good. Our actions, thoughts, and feelings either contribute to the most beneficial path for all or they take away from this greater good.

Compromising can be a useful tool. However, a compromise made without the consideration for the greater good is not a compromise at all. It is an unbalanced decision.

A compromise is a choice, conscious or not, that is seeking to ease a situation of discomfort or potential discomfort. I love having people over to my home, and my partner likes to keep the house to mostly just us, so we practice compromising all the time. I don't have people over as often as I want (situationally, this is an easy compromise because it is a trek to get out to our home), and he will also open our home when I ask. We each work together in this compromise through open communication; it can feel uncomfortable to ask because I know that my request will likely cause him some discomfort.

I reclaim my power in this situation, first because it goes against my inner people pleaser, which I know depletes my energy. Second, I practice asking for what I want and allowing my partner to have his own experience with my request. I know his response will always be, "Make the right decision," and he knows my answer is still going to be, "You know I will decide to have my loved one out." So in a way, the decision is made together. If his response were ever, "I am not comfortable with that," then I would get more precise about his choice by asking him to clarify his resistance. In the end, it is about respecting each other and intentionally listening.

Imagine your life as a balance scale. You are at the center, your personal needs, wants and desires are on one side. On the other side are the needs, wants, and desires for everything else. The goal here is to keep this scale balanced. If it is tilting in the direction where your needs, wants, and desires are outweighing the other side, I invite you to come back into balance. On the other side, if the needs, wants, and desires of everything else has more weight, then it is time to receive. What is fascinating is when you practice being in this sweet spot of balance, the liquid flow of Being, everything expands. The scale of life becomes bigger. Instead of taking away from the pie, we are growing a bigger pie. Each side has a gravitational pull to it, the weight and balance of your scale matters. Practice being in harmony.

How can the needs, wants, and desires of one be equal to everything else?

Your life does not exist without you. You are the most significant part of existence; therefore, the gravity of your value is equal to all other things. No one is better than another. We are equal.

Your soul is no less valuable than my soul. However, being in a socioeconomic class assigns a value to each one of us as humans. The scale of disparity is collapsing humanity.

The skill of keeping life in balance is developed through an awareness of **knowing what your needs, wants and desires are.** Basic requirements are shelter, food, and water. Wants are anything that makes life more comfortable or convenient, like organic restaurants. Desires are anything that beckons your energy with passionate excitement. My desire is a 100-acre ranch, resting within the mountains with a river running through it, where I create retreat experiences for individuals who want to get lost and discover the beauty of themselves and life.

Without this clarity, a compromise can be detrimental to your integrity.

Your life's natural rhythm will fluctuate in and out of harmony. The practice is expanding the harmonious times by practicing the above balancing skills. Be patient with the disharmonious times by not shunning them as something wrong. Instead, accept them as times of growth for greater balance. When you feel dis-ease, a state of not being at ease either physically, emotionally, or mentally, the scale starts to tip, and you get to choose whose needs are more significant. This choice can create its own feeling of dis-ease, especially if you are on the outer edges of the spectrum for being selfish or selfless. If you are selfish, practice selflessly giving. If you are selfless, practice sacred selfishness. These intentional choices help keep you in balance. In theory, we all want to coexist so that the greater good is the ultimate winner in all situations.

Unconscious compromises energetically acknowledge that you are willing to put others before yourself. This can be a double-edged sword. By engaging in this practice, you are affirming the importance of the other party involved, and that their experience is equal, or more important, than your own. It is also confirming that you do not know your value because this choice is lacking conscious consent, giving away your power. Compare this experience to when you make a conscious compromise, and you can reclaim your energy by being intentional with your contribution to the situation. Remain within your integrity and awareness of your energetic worth. Your compromise is a gift to the greater good, which includes yourself.

A compromise puts your value in second place and often comes from fear or love. A compromise out of fear removes the power of choice you are submitting. A compromise out of love can feel more rewarding because, ultimately, you know your sacrifice will serve the ones you love. These are the most critical times to use discernment to ensure the greater good for all.

A tool you can use to reclaim your energy from within a compromise that ultimately provides the value of safety, stability, and security is gratitude. When you are on the receiving end of a compromise, you must say, "Thank you." The simple phrase of "thank you" allows the compromising to know that their act of service or sacrifice is acknowledged and valued.

Reactive anxiety can develop from compromise when you repeat the same compromise over and over again and never receive acknowledgment or appreciation for it. For example, if you are always doing the dishes and you never receive a "thank you" for continually giving up your time for a shared household responsibility. You could quickly become bitter at the situation and blow up at your partner when the acknowledgment for your effort is not recognized.

A silent compromise will eventually feel like a sacrifice. In a relationship, if you are always saying, "It doesn't matter" when you know it does, yet you don't want to rock the boat in whatever the given situation, then you are silently making a sacrifice.

When you sacrifice your feelings to increase the value of others, you are devaluing yourself. You are giving your power away. Depleted power or self-worth will increase stress in your life. The negative self-talk will become louder, constructing an invisible prison of Modern Fear with your self-worth inside of it.

Understanding the root cause for your willingness to over compromise is the way you get to reclaim your power and rewire your subconscious patterns. It requires that you sit openly and compassionately with your hard truths. Discover why you continually choose to be a chronic over compromiser. When I went through this discovery process, I finally figured out why I was a people pleaser. I wanted to be accepted, and this led to me over compromising.

- Are you a people pleaser, fearful of rejection?
- Do you appreciate your own value?
- Do you know the power of the contribution you share with your presence?
- Why are you willing to take second place?
- How often do other's needs, wants, and desires get prioritized before your own?

If you are willing to compromise in one area of your life, where else are you compromising or sacrificing? How we behave in one area of life is guaranteed to show up in other areas of life.

Suppose you have over given by being selfless or overtaken by being selfish, knowing when to compromise sounds easier than it is because you are programmed to tilt your scale. Your plotting mind gets involved. If you are selfish, you will hear your mind making justifications for your behaviors, as the mind loves to rationalize anything. If you are selfless, thoughts like, "If I don't do this, then how will that person respond?" You imagine the worst-case scenario, which creates more reactive anxiety and a greater probability that you are going to give away your value to the other person.

If you notice this happening in your thoughts, remember the "What if" from earlier. You are never going to know "what if," so ask for what you feel you need and see how they respond. Compromising should be a practice of negotiation, not just rolling over on your back.

Remember, a compromise should be a practice of being in harmony and balance with the greater good. A well-considered compromise is an agreement for the greater good of all parties involved. It will keep you in balance on your compromise scale so that the scale will grow bigger for everyone involved, rather than tipping in favor of one party or another.

CONTEMPLATION

In the practice of contemplation, we can find our profound inner root truth through the power of acceptance, which is a reclaiming tool.

Contemplation is the practice of turning your energies inward by proactively using the mind to witness and embrace the power of merging the energies of our mind, emotions, and body, and create a heightened state of self-awareness. There is a lovely book called *The Art of Contemplation* by Richard Rudd. I discovered the book's wisdom after I had mostly completed this book's writing and was captivated by how they aligned in many ways. The book is relatively small, less than a hundred pages, yet the wisdom within could take a lifetime to digest and integrate fully. If you are interested in establishing a contemplative practice, I recommend *The Art of Contemplation*.

As we move through contemplation, we find acceptance, which is a knowing that releases you from the invisible prison of Modern Fear and leads to a feeling of relief. As you begin your quest for truth through the lens of Modern Fear, you will discover thoughts, feelings, and behaviors that no longer serve your greater good. The next step is to accept these truths, not as right or wrong, simply as **your truth**, good, bad, or ugly. This is the only way that you will be able to rewire these experiences within your conscious awareness.

Simply acknowledge and allow. This tool of acknowledgment is active witnessing and can become a practice to reclaim stability within our own being so that situations no longer cause a reaction within us. Instead, they simply are there for observation and response.

At the source of acceptance, you will find a seed of love; because you are no longer fighting against something you cannot change, fear is released by this embodiment of truth. In my healing journey with my mother, acceptance has been the tool that has allowed me to witness the hardship of what my mother's life was really like, without the projection of my heartache. I can only imagine what it was like for my mom because my lifestyle is vastly different from how she lived when I was a child. The cards were stacked against her, low socioeconomic status and single mother of four children, I can imagine that life felt overly burdensome.

It took curiosity for me to be able to release blaming my mother for the hardships of life. Once I shifted from accusation to curiosity with my questioning, I was able to discover the path of acceptance.

I was at the Best Year Ever conference a few years back, and the facilitator, Jon Berghoff, said, **"The moment we ask a question, our future is forever changed."** This statement shifted something within me, just like "two positives for every one negative." At that moment, I learned the real power of asking questions, and not the questions that hold us prisoner within Modern Fear, like "Why did this happen to me," but rather regenerative questions that create curious intrigue and life-giving energy like, "Why did this happen **for** me."

If you choose to ask a question from the perspective of, **"Why me?"** then energetic depletion is going to continue to leak out of you because we cannot change our external world without changing our inner world first. The answers that you receive to the "why me" questions will continue to contribute to the reactive anxiety and stress of Modern Fear. These questions only project blame and perpetuate victimhood.

If you ask from the perspective of the greater good to keep that scale in balance, you might be surprised at the answers you receive. The trick is listening for the answer and not prefilling your response with judgmental expectations. It was difficult for me to find acceptance for the harm done to me. I wasn't until I was able to recognize that I wouldn't be the person I am today without the harm of my past. Now, I can say that I thoroughly love myself. My strength comes from these deep wounds that directly provide me with compassion and empathy for others, rather than disgust and disdain. I understand that the people who chose to violate my rights have to live with their insecurities within shame, doubt, worry, anger, and fear; they are the ones that will carry the burden of their behaviors, not me.

There is an element of faith on the path of acceptance. It is easy to want to react in anger when contemplating and discovering acceptance.

There is no set path to this process. There is no right or wrong, and this journey is difficult. You will question the reasons as to why releasing yourself from Modern Fear even matters because to feel all of our feelings is a wild and yet rewarding ride. You will question this meandering journey through contemplation, which is supported by the faith in yourself. Have the courage to receive all messages, externally and internally, and foster a willingness to discern which answers will support your growth and which will continue to hold you within the prison of Modern Fear.

I know this path is not easy. I am inviting you to be with the difficulties that have stolen your energy; this is the only way to reclaim your energy from these experiences. To become whole, I had to discover what was broken and have a desire and willingness to be whole.

As you explore your truth, the first answers you will receive are typically attached to the current story you are telling yourself. These are surface answers. Modern Fear results from burying your feelings as a means of surviving through life, with possible moments of experiencing rewarding interactions.

If you have had reactive anxiety or excessive exposure to stress, at first, you will not be able to hear the root truth. Practice patience as you peel back the layers of your story. The anger and fear that held me, prisoner, within Modern Fear didn't just one day disappear. I began my journey first by looking at the abuse that happened to me and shifting this acceptance to "it happened for me," so that I can be healthy as I support others moving out of Modern Fear. I moved through the layer of the harm I caused others, owning my contribution to the abuse cycle and actively making a choice to support others in becoming aware of their own contribution. I then moved through death and the heartbreak of losing a loved one. This gave me a deeper appreciation for living, allowing me to see the non-essential relationships and habits that were not serving my greater good. It became easier to release the toxicity present in my life so that I could receive more joy and love. Layer after layer, I practiced contemplating experience after experience until I was able to reclaim my energy through a more profound acceptance of each situation. As the fear dissolved, I found more safety, security, and stability.

My own story is complicated, just as yours likely is; be kind and gentle with yourself, as this journey can take a lifetime and is not meant to provide an instant answer.

I would like to peel back the layers of a common triggering experience that has impacted every single person who has ever driven a car. Let's walk through a scenario like road rage, which is a stressed state of mind that contains a variable amount of anger or frustration and can be a trigger for anxiety.

Why might you or I get road rage?

The easy answer is that other drivers are idiots. However, this is a projection of my frustrations on their driving skills. Let's be real, I have yelled at the other driver for not paying attention to what they are doing more times than I would like to admit. Common outbursts I have heard myself say is, "What are you doing?" "Go!" "Hurry up." Does any of this sound familiar? I know that when I hear myself speak in this way, my feelings have become reactive. I am no longer in a relationship with my feelings, and in fact, they are controlling my reactive behavior.

Other people are not the source of your feelings; you are. This is a challenging lesson to accept; embody this responsibility to get out of the prison of Modern Fear.

So besides "people are idiots," why do I get road rage?

Perhaps I am running late and therefore have a lack of time.

A second layer, why am I running late? Do I have a tough time getting prepared to leave? Are my thoughts scattered, trying to finish up one task so that I can shift gears to the next? Do I have too much on my plate to focus my attention?

I invite you to test your listening skills, and start to pay attention to how often you say out loud, "I would, but I don't have time," "I want to, but I don't have time," "If only I had time."

Lack of time management, or overextending yourself, are major contributors to Modern Fear and road rage.

The more time you spend with exploratory, contemplative questions, the deeper truths you will find.

I have the truth of not valuing myself. I overextend my commitments, which causes a decrease in time management. Just below the surface of this truth is an even deeper one.

Do you value yourself? It seems like a no-brainer answer. However, in deep conversations, I hear more often than not, "Not as much as I should."

Stop here and soak this in. Your life does not exist without you. You are the most important person in your life. Your health and well-being should be a priority. Do you feel a resistance to this statement? Perhaps this sounds selfish to you? This would be a great time to reflect on the idea of sacred selfishness, as long as it is in alignment with the greater good.

In contemplation, I have discovered how my root truths that lead to a greater acceptance of any situation link directly to my ability to feel safe, secure, and stable. Even in the example of road rage, my lack of time management stresses me out because if I am running late for work, which can threaten my job security. I don't want to get in trouble and potentially lose my job.

In all emergency training, the first rule is to ensure your safety before helping others.

Why? Because if you are not safe, you are not in a position to provide support.

Being in a state of Modern Fear is an emergency. You are not living your life to the fullest potential, which is a life not fully lived. I invite you to make a conscious choice about how you want to live your life and accept that decision as your path of truth. I used to decide to live a life of numbing my feelings unconsciously. Now, no matter how difficult or uncomfortable a situation has become, I do not numb; I stay present so that I may become comfortable in my discomfort.

When we are witnessing buried inner root truths, and the chaos that is created by not having a relationship with these inner truths, there is the opportunity to shift our perspective. I over gave because I didn't acknowledge that I had a root truth of, "I am not enough." This lack of connection caused my energetic force to become depleted. I was getting by using the fumes of my willpower to survive. When I was able to shift my perspective, and I began to witness the value that my presence provided to others and myself, I was able to uproot the buried truth of unworthiness.

Replacing it with the potential of my value allowed me to reclaim my energy from draining situations.

Time is the greatest gift we have. We do not know how long we will be on this earth; no one does. If you accept your existence as uniquely yours and the fact that your time is finite, your life will suddenly become more valuable.

You will start to discern what is of importance to you. Practice paying attention to how you feel in situations where Modern Fear shows up, and you block the expression of your feelings.

Contemplation is a lifelong tool. The quest for truth can, and will, feel impossible at times. You will remember past parts of yourself that might bring up feelings of shame, disappointment, anger, and all of this is beautiful. It means you are hot on the trail. Don't turn back. **Be respectful and reverent with yourself and ask permission to continue.** If you have suppressed a complicated inner truth, when you open up the doors to that invisible prison, you could potentially experience it again. The degree will vary, but your mind, body, and feelings will respond.

So how do you find the healing power of acceptance?

You remove judgment. You remove your projected expectations and stop trying to control the uncontrollable.

Sounds easy, right? It can be if you listen with an open heart and a quiet mind.

THE HEART

An Ancient wisdom guides us to follow our hearts. Every time I have approached an elder with worry, they ask me, "What is your heart saying?"

When I get plagued with a tough decision, and my head can't make up its mind, I am either going to stress out, or I am going to slow down and listen to my heart. When the conversation gets too loud in my head, it is time to feel it in my heart. I know that I need to stop, put my hands on my heart, breathe, and listen.

Do you have a practice of listening to your heart?

The mind creates a chaotic world. Look around. You are living in it. There are many rules, guidelines, and regulations that must make this system work. The mind is about contrasts and comparisons, and it has been in control for a long time.

The heart, on the other hand, creates a connected world. It can open up the space of infinite wisdom. The heart never lies to you; it will always be honest with you even when it hurts. The heart is our inner warrior. It will go the distance, and it will also say when enough is enough.

When we lay our weary heads down to rest, our heartbeat is our constant partner that keeps us alive. It is the drumbeat that does not quit.

Part of the humanitarian shift that we as a society are experiencing is the opening of the heart energy. We are tired of the injustice the mind can create and manipulate. We are feeling into the deeper meaning of being human, and that energy is within our hearts.

Trapped in Modern Fear, I could not feel my heart while lost in my trauma. My mind had me so protected that I never even knew I should be able to feel my heart. It wasn't until I had my mental breakdown at 28, when I radically uprooted the life I had created, that I ever considered my feelings.

I was always on a mission. For the most part, I am a pretty driven person. I followed all the rules of the mind. I went to college, got a great job, got married, and bought a house. I did everything that society and my mind said I was supposed to do to make me happy.

For the most part, I was happy in my life. I felt safety, security, and stability because of the decisions I had made.

I met my husband while bartending a beauty event at Tiki Bob's. He was doing my hair in a fabulous faux hawk updo. He seemed to be flirting with me, which I thought was incredibly weird because I had assumed that all male hairdressers were gay. I was naïve; this is not true.

Before we started to date, late one evening, he sent me an email that confessed his feelings for me. I thought it was the sweetest thing anyone had ever said to me. I started to feel my heartwarming to him, and I was becoming twitter-pated.

Early on in our relationship, he shared with me that he wanted to have children, which scared me. Due to having endometriosis, I might not be able to get pregnant. I was terrified to share this news with him because previous boyfriends had elected to break-up with me when I shared this potential reality. One night, I worked up the nerves while driving him home. We sat in the car, I could feel my heart beating in my ears, and my mind was screaming at me, "Don't do it. You are going to ruin everything."

Tears filled my eyes, and I blurted out, "I might not be able to have children." I sat there, braced for his rejection, and what I heard opened my heart to trust. His response was gentle, "Well, maybe life is just meant to be me and you then."

He didn't love me for what I could provide for him, he loved me because of me, and that unconditional love was new for me.

I am confident my husband loved me, and that gave me a sense of freedom that I hadn't experienced before in a relationship. I felt empowered by being with him. He was the first man that I ever trusted. He was my rock of Gibraltar. A pillar that protected me from me in so many ways. He took good care of me, tending to our home, cooking me meals, snuggling me, and believing in me. He always supported me no matter what.

We also loved to party, which did cause conflict, however, it was always manageable. He was a good person, and I didn't want to lose that security.

We decided to get married and went to Vegas. It was a small wedding attended by his immediate family, a couple of my close friends, my cousin, and her mom. My friend Dan, who owned Tiki Bob's, was giving me away.

On the day of the wedding, I was feeling doubtful. I wondered if I deserved to be loved. On the way to The Little White Wedding Chapel, I had a few shots of Jägermeister to take the edge off. Dan and I were standing outside the room, and the Chaplin came to speak with us. He asked if we wanted him to say a prayer, and I told him that wasn't necessary because neither of us was religious. He looked at me and said, "Everyone can use a prayer." I told him whatever made him happy will be just fine.

He walked away, and it was just Dan and me. I could feel all the nerves racing through my body. My stomach was tight. I watched as a couple was getting married through the drive up, curious at how casually people were making a forever decision. I looked up at Dan and said, "I don't think I should be doing this."

He reached his hand over and tapped my shoulder, "We are already here. It will be fine." There and then, the decision was made, I would be getting married that day.

The service was quick. We vowed that we loved everything we knew about each other, and we promised to be each other's best friend. Then I became Mrs. Leslie. My heart felt pretty numb as my mind churned with doubt and worried about my deservedness. On my wedding night, I became sick and spent the night sleeping, while my husband and Dan gambled.

Together, we lived a comfortable, everyday life. For the first time, I was able to safely feel into my heart and allow for feelings to emerge. I appreciated the life we had created, and yet my mind was not satisfied. I couldn't imagine living the rest of my life on the path we were on. The safety started to feel uncomfortable because I had spent so much of my life in fight or flight.

I hit my breakdown when my brother and his family came to visit one weekend for the Cincinnati Bengals and Seattle Seahawks game. After a long day of drinking, my older brother grabbed me and said, "I am tired of fighting and want to surrender." It felt like I was being punched in my gut with a battering ram because I knew what he was saying. All the joy I had worked so hard to attain left me. My heart closed down, and I felt like a defeated shadow of myself again. I instantly became angry about the past that we had to endure as children. I went back into my victim identity, blaming my mother and the rest of the world for its evil.

My brother had been a long time addict, trying to deal with his life traumas, and he was confessing his desire to give up on life. This wasn't the first time that he had tried to give up. The demon of not wanting to live was a life passenger with him for a long time. Trying to love an addict is hard. You want to trust them, but you can't. You want to help them, but you can't. You want to care for them, but they will take advantage. Loving an addict is a toxic relationship, and yet you don't want to see an addict suffer alone, so compassion almost always wins. Addiction is a lonely, solitary, painful existence for the addict and also incredibly painful for the people who love them.

The idea of my brother's death shook my foundation. It took away the safety, security, and stability I had worked so hard to build. As the rage consumed me, I started to tailspin as my mind took over, racing to grasp onto a solution that would change his mind. At that moment, looking into my brother's deep, brown eyes, all I saw was pain, his life force absent. I instantly built walls around my tender heart, so I could not feel the depth of the heartbreak that news brought forward. Tears streaming, I looked him straight in the eyes and said, "Okay, I promise to take care of your family." I thought I was saying good-bye to my brother, and I couldn't imagine a deeper pain for me. At this point, I had no memory of my brother's trespasses upon me. I only knew that I loved him, and I didn't want him to suffer.

In the weeks to come, I realized in my own life. I wasn't truly happy. I had spent my life overextending my energy to relationships and situations that didn't always give back to me. I was mentally lost in the fact that I was still trying to please others so that I could feel of value. At that point in my life, I was like 80% happy. I didn't know what to do with that information, so I did what Bad Leah does, and I destroyed everything.

My heart was closed down, and my mind reactively raced as I sat outside in our driveway, the rain of Seattle coming down. I knew what I had to do. At least I thought I did. In trying to process the feelings around my brother, I had mentally turned myself into a burden to my husband. I had begun to tell myself that I was not worthy of his love. I began to believe the internal story that I was broken, and he deserved to be with a woman that could provide him with everything he desired.

When I opened the front door, I could smell the pork chop dinner. He always took such good care of me. I walked to the entrance of the kitchen, looking at him, my gut tight, and I asked him, "Babe, would you hate me if I asked you for a divorce?"

His response, "I could never hate you."

I blurted it out, "I want a divorce," and I ran to my office, slamming the door behind me. I hated myself at that moment. I had never felt more cowardly in my life.

He came in and sat in front of me, tears streaming down both of our faces. He didn't understand. How could he? I never shared my feelings of brokenness with him. I suffered within myself, not wanting to cause him any discomfort. That evening, I discovered just how much he loved me because he was willing to let me go. He didn't want to hold me back. He wanted me to be happy. It made me feel even worse for the pain I was causing him.

For months, he did try to comfort me. He still made me dinner. We would even snuggle in bed. We did all the things that provided me safety, security, and stability, except I was void of any feelings. My heart was closed down, protected in its survival armor. I didn't like myself during this time in my life. I was harming many people I loved as I yanked back my affections because I didn't believe that I deserved to feel love. My mind was in charge, and my heart was imprisoned. I made an escape plan. I purchased a one-way ticket to Nairobi, Kenya. I quit the corporate job that I had tried so hard to get. I sold most everything I owned, including our home.

On April 13, we stood before a judge; our hands held tightly together. The judge looked at us and asked, "Are you sure you are irrevocably broken?" I looked out of the corner of my eye at my husband. My heart heavy with shame as I felt all the love that I had destroyed. Shaking his head in what seemed like disbelief, he answered first, "Yes." I could feel his sadness as I turned to the judge, nodding my head in agreement.

As my departure to Africa approached, I began to soften in my heart. In my mind, I would silently beg for him to ask me to stay. My guilt of causing so much pain weighed heavily on me, and I was seeking reconciliation to ease the suffering. We lived together right up until the day I boarded the plane; he and my best friend dropped me off at SeaTac. As I went through the security line, I watched him watch me, angry at myself for the destruction I had caused him. I was the one that ruined his dreams, and yet he was the one who held me unconditionally through all of my pain. He truly is a hero in my journey. I will forever be grateful to him and his family for all of the love, laughter, and memories that they shared with me in my life.

A few weeks into traveling, I entered the small country of Rwanda. I was incredibly excited about this country because I was going to see Mountain Gorillas in the wild. What I wasn't prepared for were the emotions that were beginning to surface within me. The adrenaline of my decision to blow up my life had worn off, and I began to question, "What the fuck am I doing." I laid sobbing in my dormitory cot one night, surrounded by so many people. I was grieving the death of my old life, beating myself up for the destruction, and feeling sorry for myself all at the same time. It was pretty much one of the worst nights of my life, lost in my mind at one of the greatest pity parties of my life.

The next day, I woke up super early to begin the journey into the mountains. We hiked through open fields, thick forest, stinging nettle, and bamboo for some time before we came upon the family of gorillas. I will never forget looking into their eyes. I could see their souls; it was like looking into the eyes of a loved one. At one point in this experience, I felt my heart, and I cried tears of joy.

Joy can make you cry too.

I had never felt more open and connected to my heart up to that point. I witnessed creatures like me but not like me, which made me so curious. It allowed just enough space for me to feel immense love. An eight-month-old gorilla annoyed one of its elders and was put in its place. It walked away, laid back, and then a minute later, pounded its chest, jumped up, and started to play again. I felt I was witnessing a human interaction; however, what I was seeing was a community interaction. This awareness brought a lightness to my heart that I hadn't experienced in a long time.

My journey through the southern part of Africa was unforgettable, from the landscape to the people to the animals. I got to experience a part of human history I had never dreamed of, and I felt so good in my heart. Even with all of this wonder and excitement, I was in the worst emotional space of my life.

Tension had been building between my travel mate and me. At the end of the 83rd day of my overland adventure, we found ourselves in Port Elizabeth, South Africa, where I destroyed a loving relationship with a very dear friend. In my internal ugliness, I started to project my insecurities onto her. On the last night of being together, I got drunk and exploded at her in an angry rage. I was so hurt, mostly by myself, and I lost it. I ran away and hid in my bunk bed. I didn't know what I was doing next. My friend was leaving in the morning, and I was going to be alone in Africa in a complete emotional breakdown. I was lost in the chaotic upheaval of my mind and disconnected from my heart.

At that moment, I called the one person who I knew I could always count on, my lifelong friend Laurie, and asked her for help to get me out of Africa. In the middle of the night, she purchased an airline ticket for me to Ohio. My heart needed to see my niece and nephew, I needed to feel the love of family, so I went home to my sister Jackie, a woman with whom I share no blood, only spirit.

For one month, I stayed in Ohio, and I mourned all of the destruction I had created. In the comfort of stability, I was able to rest my overactive mind, and I was able to release all of my pent-up feelings. My heart wept until the prison I had built around it dissolved, and I was able to feel again, not just my suffering, but hope for my future.

During this month, I was able to care for my family as well, which gave me purpose. Jackie, my soul sister, had just bought her first house, and I supported her in setting up her home. I put a loving home together in which my niece and nephew could grow up. I filled my broken heart with the unconditional love of my family, and at the end of that month, I was able to return to my walkabout.

My family dropped me off at the Cincinnati airport. I boarded the plane back to South Africa, where I would spend a few days in

Johannesburg and then head to the Middle East.

It was in Cairo that I discovered a "strong heart." In a city with 40 million people, a taxi ride is basically like going on the scariest roller coaster ever. The driver was bobbing and weaving, stopping and honking, and I just sat there frozen in complete fear.

He looked over at me, pounded his chest and said, "Strong Heart. To be a taxi driver in Cairo, you must have a strong heart."

I looked at him and said, "To be a passenger in Cairo, you must have a strong heart," as I beat my chest. At that moment, I learned the gift of breathing. The chaos was so far out of my control; the only thing I could do was close my eyes, follow my breath, and feel the beating of my heart. I surrendered. My control freak side threw up her hands and decided to be a passenger of life instead of trying to control life. I trusted our combined hearts coherence at that moment and found freedom.

If the mind is too loud, it is so hard to hear the heart. The heart is a magical machine, and its energy is subtle, which requires us to pause and listen. It was when I was able to connect to my heart that I was able to reclaim the energy that had been consumed by my lack of self-worth and the destructive path that I had led myself down.

THE FORMULA

Step back for a moment and take a bird's eye view of your ability to be in acceptance.

Humans are naturally intrigued by things that are like themselves.

The law of attraction implies that you are attracted to similar energies because they are easily relatable. When you decide to let someone or something into your life, it is because of your similarities, not because of your differences.

We each observe and process new experiences in our own way. For example, 2020 is a year of transformation. Our global society has been faced with a pandemic and has also come together to stand against social injustices. The integration of new experiences happens without us having to be aware of the process. The brain handles the filtering and compartmentalizing subconsciously behind the scenes. Internally, we know if we either like or dislike the experience. A prejudiced belief is formed either in favor of or against this new experience.

It is tough not to be a cynical judge. Modern Fear thrives off judgment, along with comparison and duality. If you want to find true acceptance, evaluate the filters of your mind, which determine the judgment of your dislikes.

One of my mentor's (John Meisenbach) favorite sayings is, "If you don't like that person, you should get to know them better." This is true for everything. It is so important to evaluate; if you don't like something, ask why. You might never like that thing, but at least you know within yourself the source of discomfort. We, as a nation, have a powerful opportunity to acknowledge surfacing hidden systemic injustices. This awareness is making people uncomfortable. It should. This discomfort gives us the chance to dig into ourselves and discover the origin of these injustices. This acceptance of hard truth offers freedom to us as a society.

The first part of the formula is to get curious about your personal belief structures.

- When you evaluate your life, where do you feel the most noise or distraction?
- What pulls your attention the most?
- Are your thoughts running amuck?
- Is your environment filled with clutter?
- Does your physical body carry excess weight?

Just like having a sore throat or a cough when you are sick, there are signs or symptoms of Modern Fear, fatigue, stress, weight fluctuation, a short temper, and the decreased ability to focus.

The quality of your mind, body, feelings, and the environment in which you spend your time are little messengers for the Modern Fear symptoms that you are expressing.

Here is the second part of the formula. When you pay attention to the signs, the symptoms will resolve if you are willing to listen to their truth. You have an opportunity to be responsive to your needs rather than being reactive. Listen to your inner truth and be gentle with yourself as you discover your driving forces.

You intuitively know. All the answers you seek are already inside of you. So ask yourself, "What should I do with (fill in the blank symptom)," and then listen.

Calm your mind. Open your heart. Slow your breath's rhythm. Listen and feel.

At times the answer is easily heard; other times, it might be a more subtle feeling. If you listen patiently, the answer is there. Intuitive listening is a handy tool that requires practice.

When you react to a symptom, you either push it deeper inside in an attempt to ignore it, or you explode, often at arbitrary triggers. These self-abusive behaviors will inhibit personal evolution. Privilege is a word that we are using to explore the viewpoints of injustices. This word was extremely triggering for me because I never felt "privileged," everything in my life is a direct result of my efforts to better my existence. The trigger of this word left me blind to the injustice I was not willing to feel because of the pain connected to my shame. I was scared to imagine that other people have it worse than I did. My empathy locked away within Modern Fear.

Then, during a conversation with my dear friend Jessica, she explained to me what privilege means, and I broke. I felt into my injustices so that I could feel the mistreatment of black people and all other people who are being exploited by the system. It was a humbling conversation. I got curious about my discomfort, and I listened to my internal resistance. And what I found was a cowardly reaction within me, and that is okay. I am not judging myself. I am allowing space for this truth to become a stable foundation so that I may continue to grow as a compassionate human.

There are several ways to begin a practice of listening for signs and symptoms of Modern Fear.

First, I had to accept that I do not feel my feelings at 100% capacity. Parts of me are numb. Even now, with all the internal work I have done, I still didn't have the integrity to be entirely empathetic to injustices. I acknowledged my dis-ease rather than pushing through it or hiding from it. I allowed my mind to accept this truth so that my heart could feel more deeply.

Symptoms can be reoccurring thoughts, pains, and abusive behaviors. Dissatisfaction is a symptom that screams to be heard but requires work to change. Patience is vital when listening for signs that we receive from observing our environment. Listening to our intuition and moving from our head into our hearts. There is no easy button in this process.

The third step in the formula is to **change your behaviors from a reactive to a responsive approach.** When you become aware of a symptom, acknowledge it as a messenger of a greater truth, and appreciate this gift.

Once you are aware, it is harder to ignore the symptom, and you get to decide what you want to do with the sign.

The final step in the formula is to make acceptance a ritualistic practice.

Bring moments of attentiveness, meditation, mindfulness, and contemplation into your daily routine. These practices allow you to acknowledge signs or symptoms that have been waiting to be heard.

Get curious, listen, change your behavior from reactive to responsive, and make this a daily ritual. This integrated formula will reclaim your energy from otherwise draining situations. It will allow you to find sovereignty within your being because you will be in a more profound acceptance of your inner truths.

FORGIVENESS

To forgive is to release an energetic attachment. Heavy, darker feelings are sticky. They will attach to you because they need you to survive. This energetic field is parasitic. **When we hold back our forgiveness, we are amplifying the magnification of these darker energies.** Being unforgiving is an energy drain.

I am a natural forgiver because I am a recovering people pleaser. Of course, there are things that I still struggle to forgive. I am human.

I am not a religious person; however, I am a fan of Jesus. He was a kind person, and even as he was being crucified, he was asking God to forgive the people because they knew not what they did.

When we are not conscious of the consequences of our thoughts, feelings, and actions, we don't fully know how we impact others. In my own experience, I have found that the people who I feel have done an injustice to me or betrayed me often have no idea that they have harmed me. They lacked awareness. I also held back my feelings to not make others feel uncomfortable. For years I suffered by others' actions without allowing the other person to offer forgiveness because I didn't want to be in an awkward situation. Who does that serve? No one. Holding my voice back only causes me more harm because I am suffering internally. The person who has hurt me has no idea, and as such, can continue this abusive behavior with others.

When we do not speak our feelings, we are causing more harm than good. Words matter. The saying, "Sticks and stones may break my bones, but words will never hurt me," is a lie. Words hurt. And yet, we are carefree with our speech. Words are weapons that cause harm if they are misused.

In fact, in writing this book, my words might hurt some people's feelings. For that, I am sorry. I am sharing my experience and beliefs because I love humanity and a change in awareness is necessary. I hope that you forgive me, and I thank you for your consideration.

LEAH LOVELIGHT MICHAEL | 161

Forgiveness comes from the inside of each one of us. It is not something that someone else can do for you. **When we forgive, we are releasing our attention from the pain or anger, and we are allowing space for compassion and kindness to grow.** Forgiveness is an act of self-compassion. It is not for the other person, although they might feel a sense of relief.

The quality of our attention directly reflects the quality of our connections and external manifestations. Our attention is scattered when trapped in Modern Fear. This is why forgiveness is such a powerful tool because it releases our attention from the experiences that drain us.

When we have harmed others, and we ask for their forgiveness, we are asking to be released from the internal destruction we are doing to ourselves. I believe that as we seek forgiveness, we can often do so under the veil of trying to make a "wrong" we have done "right" with the other party involved. Ultimately, this is a by-passing because forgiveness must come from the inside to express on the outside. I have hurt others, I have asked for forgiveness, and I have been denied. At that moment, I learned that I couldn't change what I did. I will live with those consequences for as long as necessary; however, I can forgive myself. When I was harmful to others, I was destructive to myself, and I acted out of alignment with my integrity. I don't need to continue to beat myself up. Humans are the only species that will shame ourselves over and over again. In nature, when species make a mistake, they must adapt or die.

Waiting for others to say they are sorry for the harm they have caused you is depleting your energetic field. You are waiting for someone else to establish awareness, and that journey is typically difficult, not to mention long. We have to look at all parts of ourselves to become aware. A better practice might be to look within yourself and see how you have mistreated yourself because of what others have done to cause you suffering. Begin asking yourself for the forgiveness of your internal trespasses, and the desire to have other people admit their wrongdoing will begin to dissolve. This is how we reclaim our energy within forgiveness.

Focus your energy on present joy and the potential of what is next, versus the pain of what was.

STRONG ENOUGH

As a child, while at church, someone once told me that God doesn't give us more than we can handle. I remember thinking that I must have pissed God off. If God is giving me all of this, then maybe I am strong enough.

I am still confused by how we can believe we are a humanitarian race when there are so many who still lack the fundamental human rights of safety, stability, and security. This oppression that puts humans into a space of survival creates the reactionary world in which we live. Unmet basic needs make it is tough to reclaim our energy because our livelihood is unstable.

My life circumstances made me believe that I needed to prove my strength with reactionary force. I damaged relationships with myself and others. I repeatedly destroyed my safety, security, and stability because I didn't believe I deserved to feel that way. I was trapped within my mind, trying to survive within an oppressive reality.

It wasn't until I was brave enough to witness the manipulative systems that I recognized there are only a few people that receive the exuberant majority of safety, stability, and security due to greed. These corrupted people in control ensure that the majority stay on the bottom of this broken system trying to survive, while they sit on their throne, thriving in decadence. I don't want to be part of a system that takes advantage of another's disadvantaged state. I feel it is my moral responsibility to reclaim my energetic contribution to these broken systems by using my words to bring awareness to this oppression.

My views have evolved since I was a young girl going to church. I was getting the message, "you are strong enough," mixed up. I thought it meant I am strong enough to handle the feeling of loneliness. I thought it meant that I am strong enough not to need support. I thought it meant that I was strong enough to experience this crazy world of life, always feeling devalued. This might be the craziest belief that I have ever had.

"I am strong enough" doesn't come from seeing yourself as having the ability to carry the weight of the world. This belief is an energy drain. Just because you can, doesn't mean you should. This belief creates isolation, and we miss out on the opportunity to experience support, kindness, and grace.

"I am strong enough," means that you can stop and listen to why the world needs carried, and facilitate a solution that aligns for the greater good.

Listen to yourself. Your ability to hear and feel your inner truth is the only way to reclaim the energy that has been taken from you or lost. Once you are sovereign within your own being, the external stimulus can no longer control you.

SECTION 3

REWIRE

Align your thoughts, feelings, and behaviors
towards your greater good.

"The outer rests and relies upon the inner."
Richard Rudd

As energetic beings, we have an electromagnetic force field that radiates from our bodies. We have our own flow and frequency. When we shift perspectives, we rewire our electromagnetic energy field, so it is more harmonious with that which we are currently aligned.

Small shifts happen over time. Lessons we thought we have learned will come back around in different ways so that we can continue to rewire to our highest form of self. The practice of rewiring is learning to refine the quality of our attention within the cycles of the lessons.

Taking time to put your nourishment first is vital to rewire your path out of Modern Fear. What is your mind, body, and soul craving? How do these individual parts want to be nurtured?

The practice of rewiring my thoughts, feeling, and actions didn't fully start to happen until I finally reached the point of getting completely frustrated and annoyed with myself. I straddled the fence of who I used to be and the desire of who I wanted to become. I was stuck until I realized, rewiring is a moment by moment tool to be used to transition life from the old to the new ways of being. Small conscious choices are the only way to prevent backsliding into the past.

INTENTIONAL LIFESTYLE

I have found the best way to rewire my brain, behaviors, and the connection to my heart is to establish a practice that nourishes me by supporting myself first before anything else.

There are many books out there on personal development. I recommend one that changed my life called *The Miracle Morning*, by Hal Elrod. The focus of this book is on helping to develop a daily S.A.V.E.R.S. practice that puts you first. Yes, it happens in the morning. There is plenty of research on how the brain works and why the morning is the best time for taking care of you.

I feel having a committed practice to self-care is more important than the details of your practice. When I first started working with The Miracle Morning S.A.V.E.R.S, I felt like I had to do every presented step. However, what was intended as a support system instead became a space where I would crucify myself if I didn't do it all. A practice meant to give me relief ended up being a space of tension.

I adapted my practices and gave grace to myself to evolve instead of being rigorously attached to a single methodology. I decided to allow for space new wisdom to come forward. For example, I introduced things that challenge me like the Wim Hof Breathing Method. I change the type of meditations I do. Right now, I practice the Heart Lock Meditation from HeartMath. I am always in the practice of journaling. There is great power when the pen hits the paper; I put all the noise inside my head into physical existence, and it no longer consumes my energy. The only vital aspect of this practice is that you allow yourself to show up every day for yourself.

Another critical piece of rewiring is to open up to the guides you will have in your life, be that a coach, a shaman, a lightworker, a priest, or a witch. Many guides have taught me, all of whom have influenced my life in positive and negative ways (which with practice can eventually turn positive).

Like all industries, the personal development industry has leaders that genuinely are interested in the greater good of the communities they are supporting. Some leaders understand the power of manipulation and will make you feel so good you want to throw your money at them. This can be tempting because they are professional marketers and know what to say to stimulate you in positive ways that can evoke a hopeful feeling for possibility.

Be aware that if you are working with someone that is only pushing you to see the positivity and optimism in everything, they are not providing you with a holistic approach to your development. When we rewire to focus on the good in everything solely, we are limiting our ability to handle uncomfortable situations. Sometimes we need to get angry, frustrated, and sad. This is where significant changes happen. We name our anger to feel it and defuse it. I am asking you to be brave and feel all of your feelings. We need to be able to feel those more challenging feelings too so that we can express and communicate them in healthy ways.

If we choose to live in only sunshine and rainbow magic land, then when the storm comes, we will buckle under Modern Fear. I could choose to believe that reality is only the mountains that I live in and the life that I have created for myself, but that would not be honoring the greater good and being a resource to support the suffering of humanity. Once we can stand within the chaos of our being, we can become a stabilizing force in someone else's tornado.

To be a positive optimist does not mean you are perfect or better than anyone else. It does not mean your viewpoint is right. It can lead to shaming yourself when you experience more solemn feelings. To live solely in optimism is preventing you from being able to experience the richness of what life has to offer. If you have disconnected yourself from feeling the full spectrum of your emotions, this is Modern Fear. If you are only an optimist, it merely means you are not willing to experience the whole picture. This type of positivity can become negative because you become afraid of the "negative." which feeds the fear in general.

Remember, when you seek a guide within the personal development world, that a coach, healer, guide, priest, shaman, or witch can only take you on your journey as far as they have been willing to go themselves. This means that if they have never explored their shadows, they are not going to be able to support you while you excavate your own. If you feel you have peaked in your development with your guide, move on. **Don't become attached to the person supporting you.** Become attracted to the person you see within yourself that you want to nourish.

Just like all relationships, the guides that you work with should be with you for your season of discovery with them. If you have become dependent upon their services, you are not becoming a sovereign being that can support yourself. You are just looping yourself back into a dependent relationship that has plateaued. It feels safe and comfortable, but personal development happens in discomfort. It is the way we stretch ourselves to break free of the barriers within and around us that lead to life transformation. Commit to the transformation of you. Self-discovery is a journey that lasts a lifetime, and it is important to recognize that you will always be rewiring your energetic fields to become more centered within your being.

WORK AND LIFESTYLE

A lifestyle dedicated to the responsibility of your job is a life half-lived. People confuse work with purpose. The responsibility of work is something that must be done. Purpose is the expansion of your soul. It is your inner genius and the gift that you are on this earth to express.

- Is your job your primary purpose in life?
- How many times a day, when you are not at work, are you thinking about work?
- Do you check your work emails outside of work hours?
- If it does not fill your heart with purpose, why does your job occupy your precious energy? Consider that it might be taking up too much of your time.

If your career or job is one of your only identities, meaning that without your job, you would be without purpose, then your life is purely directed to external validation, and there is an opportunity to rewire the value of your time. Our purpose comes from within. It is not something given to us. It is something that we get to discover.

Most people spend, on average, at least 40 hours per week working, if not more. Forty hours per week means that you spend 24% of your week dedicated to either working for your dream or someone else's bottom-line. Are you stuck in the rat-race?

As I have shared, I pursued the American Dream, and as I write this book, I still work in corporate America for a fantastic company that I know values me. I know the perceived security of the paycheck that a job can provide. It gives me comfort that my job holds me in safety and slows me from pursuing my passion and purpose in life. In the time that we are facing right now with the pandemic which has taken our world hostage, more than ever, I am grateful for my dedication to my job. Being an insurance broker isn't my dream career; however, it has provided absolute security while I build the foundation for launching my purpose.

The amount of time your job requires and the income it provides influences your lifestyle. If you are not happy in your career, or if you are doing it solely for the paycheck, it is time to reevaluate your purpose. Dig in, be brave - what is your passion?

I found my way into corporate America because I thought it required me to become significant to others. I never gave much thought to the impact that I wanted to make in the world because I was only chasing money. I didn't have the mental ability to dream of something more, because I was merely trying to survive. I didn't have the emotional availability to acknowledge if my soul was satisfied because Modern Fear had me trapped. Once I recognized that I was being held prisoner due to the systemic influences that govern our culture, I was able to break through to my passion and purpose, which is to be a facilitator to guide others to feel the full spectrum of human life. Once we are aware, we can make a conscious choice.

My passion is to serve, love, and to support others in releasing themselves from the fear frequency. No one, and I mean no one, deserves to live a life full of fear. For too long, it has been one of the absolute worst violations of human rights.

For any of us to be able to embrace our purpose and passion, we must rewire our internal commitment to how we allocate our time and the priority of importance. If working in a job fills you up, own it, celebrate it, and rejoice that you have it. I am not against working for someone else. I am inviting you to seek passion and purpose and exercise that awareness muscle consciously.

What would it take to wake up and be excited for the day? Be honest with yourself.

Do you give away too much of your precious time to others?

DO YOU REPEL OR ATTRACT MONEY?

Fear and stress are natural repellants. So if money is stressing you out, then energetically, you are repelling money.

Do you curse money, blaming it for not being there for you? This curse is repelling money.

Are you afraid to even talk about money because of social stigmas? Your trapped voice is repelling money.

Do you dread paying your bills? This dread is repelling money.

All of these money stresses cause fear, and fear repels.

Money linked to our security contains underlying fear. This energetic connection is what holds us in prison around the heavier feeling towards money.

This tangled web of scarcity is one we all get to rewire as we move from fear of money into the appreciation of money.

Imagine our energetic connection to money as a hose used to water the garden. At first, you lay that hose out nice and straight, and the garden gets plenty of water. One day you kick the hose as you are walking by, and it puts a small kink in the hose; the garden still seems to be getting water, except it's not, and some of the plants are not growing as well because of this lack. Then imagine that this kink is there for so long that it damages the membrane of the hose, and a small leak starts. You straighten the hose again, and yet it still doesn't seem to be enough water, because now there are small leaks that you can't see draining the water before it gets to the plants. You know how important the water is to the garden, yet the tool you are using to get the water to the garden has invisible blocks preventing water's full pressure. To save the garden, you must look at the tool you are using. If your energy is out of alignment with gratitude for money, then your money hose is kinked, and you are not receiving the full nourishment.

When we move the energy of money from the scarcity fear of the mind to the heart's trust and gratitude, we rewire our relationship with money.

This is a challenging process to begin to trust because our programmed minds to react to the fear. Be gentle with yourself as you work to rewire this relationship. There is great prosperity within generosity. When we give to someone or something else, we tell the universe we believe we have plenty, we trust that we will be in abundance and have enough compassion to see that others are in need. This energetic connection will build resiliency within your money energy. To give is to receive, even if that feels backward at first, it is a universal law that exists within nature.

What if every time you received a paycheck, you jumped up and down and celebrated it. You worked your butt off for the money. Why not celebrate? Positive acknowledgment is an attractive energy.

What if every time you opened your wallet, you thanked your money for being there so that you could buy your food? This appreciation is attractive energy.

What if you delayed instant gratification and saved for an item? How would that dedication towards a purchase feel differently? Try honoring the process of consumerism, rather than fueling the addictive behaviors. This practice is a tool to be used to develop an intentional relationship with money, which is attractive energy.

Just like humans, the frequency of money likes respect for its power. When we are in fear of money, we deny its potential strength as a tool.

Fall in love with the potential of what money can do. Shift out of the fear of the scarcity that creates and reinforces the absence of money.

I have a character that I am developing within myself, **The Unassuming Millionaire.** This is the part of me that I work with to rewire my relationship with money. Ever since I was a little girl, I dreamed of the comforts of money, mostly all the food that money can buy. Now, in reality, the majority of my budget is dedicated to food. As an adult, I struggled with believing that I deserved the safety, security, and stability that money can bring. My mindset kept me in scarcity. Even though I was generating enough money, I was spending it or giving it away more quickly than I was saving it.

In my relationship with money, I discovered that I felt like people with money were evil. I feared that if I received money, greed would flaw my character. I now know these statements are true. When I dreamed of being in abundance, I would feel extreme guilt in regards to thinking about those without security. It made me feel shameful as if I was saying I was better than others, and that isn't true either.

I am not a greedy person. I am not evil, and I want to do a bunch of good with money. So I started to focus on these inner truths, which is how the Unassuming Millionaire was born. I want to have plenty of money in the bank to feel safe if the world economy shuts down. I want to be able to support others in establishing their safety and building their dreams. This requires a fluid relationship with money. I don't need designer clothing, a mansion, or a fancy car. I dream of having land deep in the woods for others to be able to come to connect with nature. I dream of getting my hands dirty while working with the land to sustain life. I dream of being able to flow the resource of money in any direction that I feel will serve the greater good, like buying my mom a home. I know I can impact most people when I honor my relationship with money because money is a considerable tool in making the world go round. Our culture has created it the way.

My desired relationship with money is to have it continually flowing to and through me. I want to be 100% debt-free, which I am currently working on. I want to have six months of savings to support my household in the event of an emergency. I want to be prepared to support myself when I am older, as I don't have children or a family to care for me when I am an elder financially. These fundamental security blankets with money will release all fear I have around money and will allow me space to rewire my energetic relationship with the money frequency completely.

Knowing what your dreams are with money is the attractive energy that will rewire your relationship to money. However, until your relationship with money is safe, secure, and stable, it is hard to dream of the potential of what money can do for you. The security of basic needs must be met to be able to dream with your money. It requires discipline and dedication because our society programs us to spend. Consumerism can keep money connected to scarcity energy and buried in material items that do not necessarily serve our greater good.

To me, being a millionaire isn't about holding all the power in my bank account. It is about acting as a channel to funnel the benefits of money back into the system so that others can feel the excitement and security of money.

Money loves to play. It loves to be spent, and it loves to transfer power. It is a significant energy and one that we should regularly interact with so that we can rewire our relationship to trust and respect with money, rather than to fear and scarcity.

THE HOPE & WANT OF DESIRE

We have learned to recognize the fears which take away the feeling of safety, security, and stability. We have reflected on ways to reclaim our energy from fear, and once our basic needs are met, we now have the energetic capacity for what else is possible.

What is it that you want?

Do you know?

Why is it that you are reading this book?

To want creates a need for something.

To hope seeds a desire.

Hope and wants can work together as a powerful tool to serve the excitement of change. However, to harness the potential energy will require action.

The specificity of your hopes and wants is an absolute requirement; any vagueness creates confusion in the fruition of your desires.

Seeing something that others have that you do not creates a want. Think about all the things you say you want; a nice house, new car, health, wealth, leisure time.

Internalize these outside forces of want and integrated to create focused attention of attainment. Move these wants from your mind into your heart and create the anticipatory feeling of what it would feel like to receive. This act of feeling is a rewiring of your energy and makes your energetic field more attractive to what it is you desire rather than what you don't want.

If you hope for your wants, it allows you to dream about them. It is in the dream where your imagination aids in building the feeling of desire. The desire you have only exists inside of you; one day, it will become the reality in which you live.

Your external world will always reflect your internal state of being.

One of the most excellent tools to support hope is to write them down. Include the reason you hope for it, and put it somewhere that you will read it every day. Record yourself reading your reasons and listen to them every day. Get your wants, hopes, dreams, and desires out of your head and put them into your physical reality. If your hopes are in front of your face all the time, it makes it difficult to suppress your wants.

As you read and hear your messages, you can feel into how your life will be when you achieve this hope. Do not worry about the steps that it might take. **Why is more important than how.** The steps will be revealed as you practice being in a relationship with your hopes. The most important part is to trust the path you are on and feel your way through it.

One hope that I have held is to be a published author. People have told me during my life journey that I should write a book. You are reading the hope that I have had for my future for as long as I can remember. Step-by-step, the process of becoming an author, has revealed itself to me. Right now, I still don't know what comes after the editing process. However, I figured it out because you are experiencing my words. I wanted to write this book because I know that the struggles I've gone through are not mine alone. I know that there are plenty of people trapped within their own Modern Fear, and this book is my sincere attempt to provide a guide to those who are tired of living within fear and want to live within love.

Focus only on the feeling. Move your wants, hopes, dreams, and desires into your heart and feel the beating of what it is like to have them close to you. Your feelings from your heart create thoughts in your mind, and your thoughts and feelings both create frequencies that will attract your desires. You feel them to achieve them. **To feel is to experience, and experience is the best way to create belief.**

Do you want a nice house? What does nice mean to you? What purpose does this nice house serve for you? What are the feelings you will have as you are in your nice home? When you pull up into the driveway, what do you see? When you open the front door, what do you smell? When you walk through the corridors, what furniture fills the space, what uniqueness of your home do you feel?

I am living in Montana's woods because while living in the city of Seattle, we dreamed of a slower, more connected lifestyle. Together we dreamed of the food we would grow, the animals we would have, and the freedom this lifestyle would bring. Our home is filled with laughter, love, play, and connection. This beautiful space started because of the desire for something different than how I was living while in Seattle.

Expand your hope into your dreams and imagination, create a desire that burns like a fire inside of you, until no blocks are preventing you from achieving what it is you want.

If there is something that you want, it means that it already exists, so get it!

That is what hope is, an attractive feeling of our imagination.

DREAMS

"I say to you today, my friends, so even though we face the
difficulties of today and tomorrow, I still have a dream."
Dr. Martin Luther King

Dreaming is a space of pure curiosity that allows us to discover all of the potential available to us at any given time. Once a dream sparks a fire within us, we can begin to foster a relationship of hope around that dream.

Dreams create excitement. They make revolution and evolution happen. Dreaming is most comfortable when the probability of success is more likely: a career, a family, and a home are common dreams.

The beauty of a dream is they can be anything that fills you with anticipation of obtainment. Your thoughts only limit your beliefs of what is possible, so open your thoughts and witness your dreams' growth.

The dream of wealth will vary in quality and quantity from person to person. $10,000 per year might seem like a fortune if one is living on governmental assistance, whereas six figures a year might not feel like a lot of money when you think in millions. No dream is too small or too big. The act of dreaming is the action that will rewire your energy to become more attractive to the things you desire. It is the practice of dreaming that is important, not the attainment.

The dream of fame or the desire to have followers or fans is unique to the individual. You might only want to be seen by your family or community. Others might dream of fame and being center stage. If one person looks up to you, then you are well-known to someone, and they will follow you because they trust you. Acknowledge the leadership you shine into this world, big or small; this is attractive energy when you are dreaming.

I know when my basic survival was lacking, my dreams consisted of safety, security, and stability. It wasn't until those basic needs were satisfied that I could dream of the wants linked to my core values of love, trust, integrity, and truth. Now that my external world reflects my internal state of alignment, I can dream of what is else is possible. I can reach into my desires and discover what feels attainable or the discomfort of what feels just out of reach. This resistance can be a powerful tool to work with to build confidence. Dreams build on each other. We often want to jump to the grand vision's finish line, but then we miss the foundation's vital building blocks that support the dream. One brick at a time is the way you build a building; the same goes for your dreams.

You can support others in their dreams, too, without even knowing what their plans are. Recognition of someone else's dream can be as easy as telling someone they are fantastic, and they are on the right path. We each want our dreams to be accepted because that energetic connection creates more potential energy for all of our dreams to come true. One of the best tricks or tools that I use when feeling discouraged in my own dream is taking a break from my own and giving energy to someone else's dream. Dreaming is best done in collaboration and support. To believe in someone else gives energy into believing in ourselves. It is a powerful tool of reciprocity. **Feed the dream that feeds you, and rising tides will lift all ships.**

The desire and need for recognition are either at the front of your mind or buried. Somewhere deep down inside of you, and somewhere deep down inside of me, we want to be witnessed for who we are.

I dream of the day that we don't have to filter ourselves or put on a mask to be someone else. If we can not be witnessed for who we are, then what is the purpose of being? Pay attention to your dreams. Are you dreaming of basic needs or wants that would bring more comfort into your life? Or perhaps, you are dreaming of your desire to change the world. No matter where you are, honor that and build on your dreams from there.

As you connect deeper into your dreams, the presence of doubt is what we are rewiring. Doubt is naturally going to occur; on the other side of doubt is recommitment, which is a powerful way to rewire your connection to your dreams.

As hope grows, so do your dreams.

Hope is a feeling that begins with inspiration, imagination, dreaming, and curiosity. The sense of hope creates the possibility of action, a dare to dream, a seed of courage to expand beyond where you are now.

When we are in a struggle for the most basic survival needs of food, water, and shelter, hope can be just outside of reach; we are too trapped in the primal survival brain to spark expanded thinking. There was no way that younger Bad Leah could have hoped to have a retreat center with tiny homes someday. I couldn't access that type of potential because I was still trying to survive.

Hope is a scary feeling if you are a prisoner of Modern Fear because it is so fragile, and yet it is mighty. Hope is a catalyst for change, and change is what must occur to be free of your Modern Fear.

Hope comes from inside of you and shows itself in many ways. Your thoughts might drift to a new idea, one that is lighter and more liberating. It is the simple act of having an idea that pushes out small frequencies of a new thought process that will attract more of the same feelings.

Witness where hope exists within your life. Make a physical note of what you hope for, big or small. This practice supports rewiring your connection to expect these outcomes so that when doubt comes in, it will quickly leave. Hope is an element of faith and trust. When we hope, there is a powerful surrender that the universe has your back. Believe that your hopes are on their way. Look for synchronicities that affirm these hopes. Once you plant the seed of hope, the timeline is to be determined by your actions when you receive the fruits. It will depend on if your mind takes over with doubt or your heart surrenders to the undeniable internal knowing.

ACTION

Hope is important because it makes you think and feel for the probable future filled with a better quality of life.

It is important to remember that action is required in manifestation. If you remember the law of attraction, like attracts like, which means, the more action you put into your dreams, the quicker they will become a reality. I do agree with the law of abundance, in that the universe will always provide. I do believe that in order to receive, your thoughts and feelings must be aligned so that you are broadcasting your energetic frequency to attract what it is you want. And, I also believe the most attractive way we can show up is through our actions. This is the rewire. We can dream and feel all we want, but until we put physical action towards our dreams, our internal desires will not become real.

Change doesn't happen overnight. I have been working on writing this book for years; every time I sit with my computer, I am putting in the necessary action in order to manifest and solidify my dreams of becoming an author.

It is critical to notice when you achieve moments of success. For example, the simple act of typing out these words demonstrates that my actions are in alignment with my dreams. When we acknowledge all achievements, big or small, we are rewiring and deepening our connection to our dreams. Ignoring successes undermines the reward of accomplishment.

When successes are not celebrated, you are telling yourself that improving yourself is not that important. We can get so caught up in the do-do-do energy that we forget to acknowledge what we have done, and looking backward to review action connects us even more deeply to the energy of manifestation. When we hurry to get to the finish line, we are missing an opportunity to honor what is working great, which is an important reflection process to support us in achieving the next steps with more ease.

LEAH LOVELIGHT MICHAEL | 183

The actual act of reaching your goal is not the part that really matters for future successes. It is time you take to acknowledge your victory of achieving your goal that provides tangible proof that you can build upon in the future. Integrating and celebrating the steps that lead to success matters for future manifestations because you are programming yourself to embody success.

Celebration is a big indication of what is important. If you find that you have made an accomplishment, but you don't feel like celebrating yourself or the energy you had to extend to reach this achievement, then this might be a great indicator that you are on a path that is out of alignment for you. Celebration allows us to continue to do internal checks within ourselves to ensure we are still moving towards a dream that matters to us. The act of celebration is the rewiring process. Our mind wants the achievement, and it is our heart that wants to celebrate the joy of the journey.

To fully recognize that you succeeded in your goal, you get to acknowledge the fact that you hoped for the outcome. Review the steps that you took to get there, and most importantly, continually evaluate if the goal set by your past-self is still relevant to the person you are today.

Your goals are the direct result of what your past-self believed was achievable. The fact is, goals that are set today are set with the intention that our future-self is still going to have the same perspective as the person we are today.

Regular reflection of your goals is necessary to confirm that they are still in alignment with the person you were when you set the goals.

Goals should evolve as you evolve. If you review your goals and conclude they no longer align with your present or future self, then rewire the goal to fit the person you are today. In theory, this rewiring should align with the probable person you want to be tomorrow. If you are not able to rewire the goal to find alignment, then perhaps the goal should be dropped altogether.

When we hope for something that is outside of our past self's perspective, then these goals can feel impossible because there is no reference of understanding within our self to base it on. There is only hope and faith in yourself that you can achieve beyond what your past self believed could be possible. Surrendering to this internal knowing connects us deeper into our intuition and supports the rewiring of moving from our mind into our heart.

THE HOUSE OF MIRRORS

In our journey through Modern Fear, there will come a time you walk down a path of mirrors. You will begin to see each person in your life as a reflection of yourself. You reading this book means that I am your mirror, and you are my mirror.

The qualities that you love about another will begin to glow and grow within you. Alternatively, you could see parts of yourself that you do not appreciate reflected in others. To reclaim your energy from Modern Fear, you get to practice experiencing what you are not allowing yourself to feel. This starts to amplify when you recognize reality is reflecting what it is time to see to get closer to all of your feelings that deserve to be free.

As you learn to rewire your focus, you will begin to discover the external world reflects your internal state of being. This is a powerful rewiring tool because it allows you to quickly notice external stimuli that you can now take ownership of and change them from an internal approach.

One of the best ways to see ourselves is to look at the world that is surrounding us. It is all a reflection. When I was numbing my feelings, life reflected many opportunities to numb. The bar was my playground. And Vegas. While discovering my spirituality, I ended up living deep in nature and in a relationship with people who are more connected to the invisible force that unites us all. When people see beautiful qualities within me, I try to acknowledge that potential within them as well. When I don't resonate with someone in a triggering way, I am fully aware that something within me is, or has been, out of alignment. This recognition allows me to become curious within myself to learn the lessons of the trigger, which will enable me to reclaim my energy from this situation.

Everything you are experiencing is a reflection of you. Your thoughts, feelings, and actions are energetic forces that are always expanding, radiating, and replicating. This reflection means whatever you consciously or unconsciously choose, it will return to you.

LEAH LOVELIGHT MICHAEL | 185

Our reflections can be triggering. We tend to avoid looking at the part of ourselves that we do not like to see. When you are standing in front of a mirror, getting ready to go out on a date and you have a massive pimple on your face, what do you do? I know I try to make it disappear. I don't want that flaw to be in my reflection.

I have already admitted to you about my relationship with dishonesty. I tried to manipulate reality to give it a lens of what I wanted others to see or believe. I know that lying started as a form of defense. I mostly lied because I didn't want to be left out or feel like I was different.

Then I got lost in the lies. Liars always do. Manipulation is a tangled, messy web, and it will suffocate the soul. When my reality gave me an opportunity to practice listening to myself talk, I noticed all of my lies, exaggerations, or omissions. Lying ended up eating me alive.

Then I learned the lesson: **where I do something once, I do it everywhere.** It was eye-opening to recognize when I started noticing the dishonesty in others and how accepting I was to their lies.

I don't want to be a liar in any part of my life. I want to have the courage always to speak my truth, and that is terrifying. I learned to listen to the words I was saying and feeling them before they are spoken. I learned to experience my body when I was lying and the feeling of discomfort that happens. I will stop myself, no matter where I am, and say, "That is not true." **I own my dishonesty;** whether intentional or not, then I speak the truth. It is a pattern interrupt, replacing old habits with new intentions until new intentions become programmed habits. This is how you change your frequency. You learn to stay centered within your integrity, and you reclaim the old energies from when you were out of alignment.

To do deep inner work, you do not have to look too far. The reflection you see can be both positive and negative; both can be difficult to own. We become unified within a stabilizing force when the reflections are equalizing rather than polarizing. We can feel like a part of our being, rather than separated from it. And that reclaims our energy because we are meant to experience life within unity.

The house of mirrors can literally be the mirror that is hanging in your bathroom. Go and look into your own eyes and discover what you see. For so long, shame was all I could see. It made me not want to look at myself, and for most of my life, I didn't.

To look deeply into our own eyes, we get to glimpse our soul. Be gentle with yourself if you try to do this. The first time I attempted to look into my own eyes, it deeply saddened me because I felt all the shame I had been projecting on myself. Eventually, I began to see me as a person, and a tenderness towards myself began to be reflected back at me. Being able to see yourself in everything truly is a beautiful existence.

CONSCIOUS REALITY CREATION

This section is a tool for declaring and rewiring your reality, the way you experience life.

Many successful people will share that one of the powerful tools they used to achieve their success is the use of affirmations: making an emotionally charged declaration as if you have already achieved your wants, hopes, dreams, and desires. I would like to point out that many times when we hear the word success, our mind automatically goes to career; however, I believe a successful life includes much more than a career, and as a reminder, I have included how I redefine success. I would invite you to take a moment and again reflect on how you define success. This is how I personally define success.

SUCCESS REDEFINED – Living life well, full of experiences without reservation. Being able to feel the intensity of the vibrational frequencies of my feelings to confirm my actions align with my greater purpose.

An affirmation is a way of saying I hope for (fill in the blank), **connecting the desired outcome to an emotion that you read and write over and over again while being present to the feeling.** For example, an affirmation that I have used while writing this book: "I am the published author of Modern Fear, which will be released in 2020. The birth of this book makes me feel excited with anticipation. It fills my heart with gratitude for the efforts I put into its completion and the release of its powerful message to inspire humanity to move from the fear frequency." I attribute this affirmation in supporting me in completing this goal.

Use affirmations to remind you to hope for your dreams!

The most amazing part about hope is that there are no limits. **Hope, combined with action, is a key to your freedom.** Through your imagination, there is no limit on how far you can go. Using your imagination with hope as your guiding light makes the improbable seem possible. You reading these words is an example of something I have hoped for that has required action on my part to consciously create the reality of this book.

> "To make this journey, we'll need imagination, but imagination alone is not enough because the reality of nature is far more wondrous than anything we can imagine."
> Neil deGrasse Tyson

When you hope for change, you have the opportunity to evaluate the nature of your current reality. Change is moving from A to B. A smooth transition is supported by understanding how you arrived at A and knowing precisely where B is.

If you are not fully aware of your energetic bond to your starting point A, that bond can hold you in that pattern. You might have to learn the lesson again, in a different way, until you can release and clear that energetic connection. For example, as I moved through my life's trauma experiences, I was never consciously aware of the abuse from my brother. I consciously processed my energetic connection to trauma and being a victim of one predator at a time. When the memory of my brother surfaced, it shocked me, and I was traumatized again. I was put back into that victim cycle to learn again that I am not a victim. I remembered that I am a powerful survivor and a leader in releasing traumatic bonds within our collective consciousness. The truth of your current reality does not have to be held in Modern Fear. With a little bit of self-evaluation, acknowledgment, acceptance, forgiveness, love, and compassion, your fears can be liberated for their next evolution, which will support your greater good. The meaning of truths can evolve.

What happens in the transition from A to B is unknown. It can look different all the time. Use affirmations as a bridge from your current reality to the future reality that you desire. There will always be unknown variables when it comes to hoping for a different situation. This is why the idea of change can be challenging.

I was having a conversation with a friend and said to him, "I think people have a hard time with change." His response was, "People don't have a hard time with change. They have a hard time with the transition." I couldn't agree with him more.

The quality of connection to my hope, wants, dreams, desires, and imagination have supported me through my energetic transition to consciously manifesting my reality. Get curious! **Curiosity is expansive energy and a tool for disrupting old habituated patterns.** When we are transitioning from A to B, curiosity helps observe energetic bonds to the past that are trying to come forward. This allows us the opportunity to determine if these bonds are serving us or holding us anchored. Curiosity also supports listening for truths that are trying to be liberated from within you, shifting surfacing anxiety to a potential opportunity.

Applying the tool of curiosity can lead to the greatest amount of growth; if used with play and wonder, it could be the tool used for a quantum leap from the person you were yesterday to the person you could be tomorrow.

To move through your transition with ease, clearly define your intentions. Root them in love and compassion for the greater good, and watch the wonders unfold.

THE EBB AND FLOW

Life is not linear. There are ups and downs, ebbing and flowing between highs and lows. This is the cycle of transition. Life is energy. You are energy. This world is energy. Everything that is made up of matter is energy. The vast expanse of space is energy.

Your willpower, attention, and intention will influence the frequency of your energy.

Your willpower is your intrinsic energy. It is the essence of your potential. Billions of molecules make up your body, each vibrating at a different frequency, influencing each other. Your body is a symphony of cells working together in collaboration to conduct the orchestration of your physical expression and your willpower. As we move from recognizing where energy is blocked to reclaiming the power that was held prisoner, we also rewire our willpower. The transition out of Modern Fear into liberation is an evolution that builds on itself, which means **every time we consciously shift out of fear, we are rewiring our willpower.**

The potential of your energy is limitless. It is a frequency that will attract similar energetic frequencies into your life. If you put two tuning forks next to each other and strike one, its vibration will cause the other to vibrate. Energy travels; it never dies. Energy is only transmuted or transformed.

What occupies your attention will act as an energetic magnet, pulling energy towards you. Your focused attention is your present reality; it equates to the quality of your life. If you are distracted, living in a fog of confusion, or simply have a difficult time focusing, you will find your life in chaos. If you focus your attention on the negative in life, then your life will be filled with dis-ease and difficulty. If you want the quality of your life to change, then rewire the quality of your attention to fine tune your focus. Your attention is a micro-loop within the bigger picture of your reality that you can use to keep on track of your desired path.

Intentions are the embodied potential energy of your mind, body, and soul. You commit to the intentions you set. Your words, behaviors, thoughts, and feelings all contain an intention.

You have intentions within your hopes, dreams, and desires that you want to manifest in your life. Your dedicated intention is creating your conscious reality, and your ability to focus your attention is an energetic force that allows for the intention to grow.

What is your intention with your **physical body**? What type of relationship do you want to have with it? Do you intend to let yourself age and your physical body decline, or do you intend to take a proactive approach for the health of your body?

What are your intentions with your **mind**? Do you intend to let your mind fall away with the complacency of passive screen time? Do you intend to keep your mind sharp, challenging yourself to learn new things?

What are your intentions with your **soul**? Do you believe in life after death? Do you have faith in an unknown force? What do you intend to do to increase your spirituality or connection to Source?

Your intentions act like transmitters for the creation of your reality. One of the most important things you can do for yourself is to establish clear intentions. Focused thoughts, feelings, and behaviors will be your conduit to the future for which you are hungry. They also act as a boundary for experiences that no longer serve your greater good.

There is a tipping point for your energy, where your focus, habits, behaviors, feelings, and thoughts will change. When I first started changing my relationship with food, I found it easier to justify an occasional fast food treat. The further I moved down my path with eating whole foods that nourish my body, the less attracted I was to fast food. Eventually, the scales tipped for me, and now I only eat convenient food on extremely rare occasions. And there are certain establishments that I no longer see as offering food but rather serving poison. I no longer identify with the old me. That person feels like a stranger in many ways, a distant memory of what once was.

This is the ebb and flow of life, the cause and the effect of your existence. **You will always be where you are.** You have a choice to stay there; this could be all that you ever want in life. You might look around and know that things must change, but are unclear on how to make that transition.

As the world evolves, so shall you. Your life is an evolution of your thoughts, feelings, and action, the connection between your mind, body, and soul.

Life is meant to be lived in ups and downs, in joy and sadness, in love and fear. The dark is necessary to know the value of the contrasting power of the light.

The birthright of being human is the gifts of your feelings, a body to experience the world, and a mind to process the lessons of life.

The acceptance and understanding of your feelings, combined with being curious about your truth, are the tools that you will ultimately need to be able to flow with the frequency of your existence and not to resist spaces of discomfort.

Learn to understand that "bad" things are bad, "good" things are good, and both are meant to be because we experience life in duality. As we become centered within the ebb and flow, practice non-attachment and find neutrality in the knowing that there is no absolute right or wrong, there is just the opposite from where you are. It feels "good," or it doesn't. Align with the greater good for guidance. Remember that we all have our part to play in this game of life, and sometimes discomfort needs to happen so that we can grow.

As we practice surfing within the ebb and flow of our energetic bonds, it is important to recognize that we are also rewiring our internal truths; connecting more deeply to be centered within our greater human experience.

A truth is true, as long as it is believed to be true. Our inner truths determine the energetic potency of our willpower, the quality of our attention, and the intentional force behind our focus. When two people share a truth, be it similar or opposite, an energetic bond is being created between these exchanges. This energy will become a collaboration of perspective, a living frequency of its own. When our energies become connected through these types of bonds, it is important to recognize what is yours and what is not. This energetic bond creates its own ebb and flow that will continue to allow you to rewire your extended energy within your personal integrity and alignment.

The process of collaboration creates a collective reality where individuals can learn and grow together, ultimately forming a collective truth. This is how, together, we rewire humanity.

We are all creators, conducting a harmony on the backdrop of reality manifesting the art of life. One symphony meshed with another to create the orchestration of the whole of existence.

A person that is unwilling to see another perspective is not being truthful to themselves; there is a fear that is clouding their lens and holding them prisoner within their insecurities. What is the harm of imagining someone else's viewpoint, as long as no harm is being caused while choosing to either agree or agree to disagree? Modern Fear prevents an open mind, a perspective that is resistant to change; it prevents the ebb and flow of energy because it is an energy block. You do not have to accept someone else's thoughts, feelings, or actions as your own. You have the free will to self-evaluate each situation as being acceptable to you or just another curious thing to experience. All interactions, big or small, are your reflections waiting to be witnessed by your energetic awareness.

The power of being able to understand or see someone else's perspective, to learn to accept other people's truths for what they are, something that is true to someone else, is a powerful tool for liberation from Modern Fear.

You will no longer feel the need to conform or change. You will be able to listen and ask questions to understand more deeply why they are committed to their beliefs, and you will be able to decide if you want your energy to flow with them or ebb away. Exploration of others will increase the understanding of yourself. You might discover beliefs from your past that are no longer representing the current truth. A potent pattern interrupt is to acknowledge within yourself, "That's not true." In fact, you might discover a deeper alliance with your faith, which will allow for more sovereignty within yourself to ebb and flow with the changing times.

The future of interacting with someone else is unpredictable. That is the beauty of interaction. What are you creating with the ebb and flow of your energy?

194 | MODERN FEAR: THE INVISIBLE PRISON

As Americans, we are facing the fact that our country was and still is built on the back of racism and socioeconomic injustices. We are supposed to be the land of the free, yet culturally, we have turned a blind eye to those still suppressed and oppressed by corrupt people in power. I do believe that this collective truth needs to be rewired. I believe that there is a time for a change, and the rage expressed right now is necessary to shock our cultural system. I stand within a strong boundary around racism and socioeconomic injustices. I witness the insecurity of those that feel threatened by the potential of what equality could look like; those individuals are being held prisoner within Modern Fear. They are living within a reactive, scarcity mindset. This prevents them from feeling the depths of the injustice used to build our country.

Each person has their own reality they were born into, which established the beliefs that ebb and flow their energy. The power of change happens within collaborative conversations, not the use of brute force. I believe that it is my responsibility to build the courage to express my willpower, to define my intention of transforming fear with love, and to focus all of my attention on the ebb and flow of healing energy. I hope that humanity evolves; what a sacred transformation to witness.

CLEAR CONNECTION TO EXPECTATION

Expectations are developed within the first few interactions with someone. Imagine meeting a new person at a dinner party. They are calm and quiet, and you enjoy them. You make plans to hang out again, one on one. Once you connect, this person can't stop talking; the conversation is all about them. Shocked by this radical change in behavior, you become uncomfortable because this person has not met your expectation of the quiet person you met at the dinner party.

Expectations can prevent joy in the present moment, either by projecting outcomes about the future or reliving the disappointment of the past. Expectations are unreliable. Unless clearly defined and shared with specific intentions, they prevent feelings of safety, stability, or security, because there are too many unknown variables.

To rewire expectations, we practice trusting our gut by not ignoring past and present situational behaviors. If other people are part of or are meant to contribute to a specific outcome, we get to practice clear communication without a complete projection of our ideas and assumptions onto a situation.

Give grace to the uniqueness of each situation. You are the one that establishes the "always" mentality. Give up this assumptive approach. Yes, history does have a way of repeating itself; however, you are in control of your own life and the way you feel and respond. If you choose to take a new perspective, you can change how history will impact today. We are doing this right now with the evolution of humanity around racism and proclaiming that this is the last generation for this limited belief, which has been crippling the flow of humanity's Source energy.

When you allow your inner judgments or pity party to project expectations, you are setting yourself up for disappointment. If someone saddens me, it is my programmed response to expect an apology, and if they don't feel they have done something wrong, then I am setting myself up to be bummed out when I don't receive my expected outcome.

When we do not allow each experience to be a new experience and approach new experiences in a repetitive way, we are being caught in a hamster wheel of the same old story. Humans are programmable beings. Habituated behaviors feel safe, leading to us feeling more stable and secure. This autopilot programming prevents us from fully allowing new experiences to be without conscious or unconscious expectations.

Thoughts, behaviors, and feelings will repeat once set in motion unless there is an active choice of change. We will show up the same way each day, which makes it easy to conclude that everyone else does the same thing. This is a contracted system of belief that prevents the flow of our energy. Any person that has done any sort of personal development or inner self-work has been faced with people in their lives that will hold them to the standard of their old, programmed patterns instead of who they have become.

In addition to having expectations of others, we have most certainly created expectations of ourselves. Perfectionism is an expectation that we are not allowed to fail or be seen as wrong. This constricted expectation of self can prevent many great things because it holds us back. The pressure to meet our own expectations will either turn us into a diamond or debilitate us in fear of judgment and disappointment. I am a person who expects a level of respect for myself, my community, and Mother Nature. I put an extreme amount of pressure on myself to do the "right" thing, and there are times that I must give myself grace. When I first moved to Montana and witnessed the limited recycling program, and I had to throw away the glass, it made me sick because I know there are solutions that are just not available to the area in which I live. We have hundreds of glass bottles in our garage because the lack of recycling options doesn't make sense. We plan to upcycle the bottles and turn them into candles; one day Lovelight Candle Co. will be born!

A tool for rewiring our expectations is our imagination. Imagine integrating and incorporating an expanded belief that **life starts over with the start of every new day.** Each time you open your eyes, you have the opportunity to be a new person. By definition, you already are. Each experience or event that you process influences your perspective; you are a constantly evolving being. This means that each interaction is new.

Rather than assuming your day will be on repeat, you get a chance to explore.

- Who will you meet?
- Where will you go?
- What makes you happy, angry, or sad?
- What experiences can you create?

Another rewiring tool for expectations is developing a **practice of appreciation** for new experiences by creating a childlike curiosity for life and the understanding of self. **Celebrate your firsts. Big or small, they are unique experiences and deserve celebration.** This is one of my favorite practices that keep me feeling fluid in life. The first time I do, see or feel anything new, I stop and acknowledge that new existence in my life, and I celebrate the fact that I have lived for many years, and life still brings new things to appreciate. This practice of celebration and appreciation keeps me out of my habituated and contracted energy and keeps me deeply in tune with the river of life.

Expectations are an illusion of control; they make us believe we are controlling a situation, and yet the expectation itself is controlling us. They become a killjoy in life unless everyone agrees with the shared expectation. Even within our own being, we can develop expectations that are too burdensome and can weigh us down instead of supporting us forward.

The best way to demonstrate your expectations is to live by the example of your beliefs.

If you expect people to be courteous, you can't tell people that they should open doors for others, but you can open the door for them every time.

If you expect people to work hard, you can't tell them to work hard, but you can put in the focused effort and improve your own outcome to inspire other's efficiency.

If you take your expectations of self and behave as a role model, then your character creates intrigue and inspiration for others. If you take your expectations and project them outward and expect others just to get it because you told them so, an invisible prison of disappointment will be built.

In my quest for joy, release from Modern Fear and self-evolution, I discovered an expectation of happiness for others. I want people to be happier. Happiness feels good, and everyone can use a little more happiness in life. But I can't tell you how to be happier; if that worked, then the world's problems would be solved. And you can't tell me how to be happier, either. Happiness is an internal discovery; I can't expect everyone to be happy. What I can do is invite you to find joy in each moment.

I love to challenge myself to live by example. When people point out to me that a behavior doesn't serve the greater good, I change it. My best friend is concerned about the way we treat our planet; she always has been active in recycling programs and waste conservation. One day we were in a conversation, and I told her I am doing my part, "I recycle." She pointed out to me that before recycle comes reduce and reuse. At that moment, I realized that I was not even close to meeting my own personal expectations, nor hers when it came to environmental awareness. Since that conversation, I haven't purchased paper towels. I now use cloth and do laundry every week, washing my reusable towels. I also haven't bought a Zip-Lock bag. I currently use the bags that come with already purchased items, like the ones your tortillas come in. And you better believe that when I get something in an actual Zip-Lock bag, it feels like Christmas to me. I haven't purchased any plastic Tupperware because yogurt and sour cream and so many other foods come in reusable plastic containers that will last a lifetime. These are the little things I do, trying to lead by example of how I feel we should treat Mother Earth. I do not project my expectations onto others. I simply demonstrate that a new way of living is possible.

It is important to be a mentor, not a dictator.

If you want the world and your surroundings to be a certain way, take the first step and live by example, no matter what other people are doing.

OWNING THE POWER OF YOUR VOICE

To share our voice gives a sense of empowerment. I heard the other day in a documentary, "I don't teach. I talk about things I care about, to those who are interested." Hearing this made me realize that people are captivated by the words that we speak. They are either inspired to learn, triggered and closed down, or neutral to the noise.

Words create our world. This understanding will have a profound impact on the rewiring of your reality because you will start to understand that everything you say, inside your head or out loud, dynamically alters your reality. If your world is chaotic, listen to the words you are speaking. Pay attention to the words inside and outside of your head.

I believe that most people are interested in being a better version of themselves. I feel this common intention among each of us, and yet, fear of the unknown comes with change. We can resist what we intuitively know is better for us. Most people have ideals that they would like to see the world share. These feelings are at your internal core, the source of your power coming forward. It is your delivery that creates the change: clear communication and leading by example is key for the ease of transition.

When you share your position from a space of love, understanding, and clearly defined intentions, it allows you to respond to others and their opinions rather than reacting to their opposition. As a society, we are faced with the opportunity to have extraordinarily uncomfortable and potentially challenging conversations because we are witnessing a true divide within our American culture. There is rage and reactive energy, which is understandably justifiable. We have lived in a nation of injustice for hundreds of years. The true evolution of this injustice will come not from the violence but the compassion of humanity.

Think about it. Why does one person value something so much, and another person doesn't seem to care one way or another about it? It all has to do with how you arrived at the value of the idea. Humans are millions of individual operating systems, and each one of us has a unique value system,

200 | MODERN FEAR: THE INVISIBLE PRISON

which can make living an intentional life challenging at times. When I walk down the road in pristine nature and see litter, it boils my blood. To devalue nature is so far away from my value system. I can't understand that action, and yet, every fishing season, it is inevitable that tourists will throw candy wrappers, beer bottles, soda cans, cigar packaging, and many other things out their windows. In my opinion, this is pure disrespect, and to others, it doesn't even register as being wrong.

I have extreme passions about things that other people do not. I am obsessed with knowing where my food comes from, and even though it terrifies me, I think about learning to hunt. As a species, we started off being hunters and gathers. We never took more from the land than we needed. With modern society and cities' inventions, hunting and gathering became obsolete for the majority of city dwellers because meat could be conveniently purchased. As an empath, animal cruelty has always bothered me. If you have ever had the opportunity to witness how commercial livestock is raised, fed, and slaughtered, I hope you would agree; it is cruel. Not to mention the contribution that the cattle industry makes to our environment due to water waste and methane production ramping up the greenhouse effect. My solution to eliminate cruelty and support Mother Earth was to stop purchasing commercially raised meat. I also considered becoming a vegan, although that isn't high on my list yet.

Hunters visit the animal in their territory. They get to see the serenity in which the animals live their life. It is hard not to fall in love with the majestic power of nature. I believe hunting would give a deep knowing of the value of an animal's life before ending it to put food on my table. There is a greater energetic value to the meat, and the energy it will provide has a deeper meaning beyond just calories to burn. There is a knowing that I can provide and support my own life through a relationship with the food I eat.

There are a lot of people who would never dream of hunting. Believe me. When I tell people, the look in their eyes is absolute shock! Their response is, "I could never kill anything" or "I don't want to cause suffering."

This is where it becomes important to provide people a clear understanding of your values. The best way to create clear intentions and support others opening up to your perspective is to use your words proactively and constructively, not a reactive and constrictive way.

In the above example, a more proactive approach to sharing my intentions would be, "I think about hunting because I understand the energetic exchange of food and want to have a purer relationship with my energy. The animal products we purchase in a grocery store come from slaughter. Animals hunted in nature are a natural part of our food chain. There is honor in their death because instinct is involved."

If people want to know more, they will ask, but typically extreme opposing beliefs will prevent a person from wanting to interact or will trigger them into reaction. When interested people engage in conversation, we learn a little bit more about each other. I often walk away with an idea I want to explore more of in the future, be it hunting, or learning more about the reality of American history.

My extreme statement, which is my truth, allows me to expand my knowledge by listening to people talk about things that interest them. I am gaining my knowledge from the ultimate source: people who already hunt or who are thinking about hunting. People will only have a conversation about something that interests them.

If your perspective is in opposition, or too far out of a comfort zone, the brain will naturally shut off. The unknown can be scary, and we all understand that Modern Fear holds us prisoner if our safety, security, and stability are not fully supported.

The hardest part about this simple idea is not feeling rejected when people do not relate, and not feeling judged when they feel the opposite. This is the rewire within our voice, being able to have an awareness of potential misunderstandings with others. As long as you align with your values behind an internal belief, you do not need validation from others. Self-validation is the rewire, and our inability to self-validate will hold us prisoner, within Modern Fear. If you practice releasing judgment based on people's reactions, you will reclaim extended energy and rewire your energetic field. Surrendering into a flow state enables an acceptance and objective witnessing of uncomfortable situations.

You can observe the interaction, ask the question, "Why am I judging myself based on this person judging me?" You will have the opportunity to respond with kindness to the person or ask questions about how they feel. You gain a clear perspective on the conversation. Indubitably, you will end up with better acceptance as a result.

If we all spoke from the heart, a place of love and understanding, with clear intentions and self-acceptance and the ability to have a bold curiosity with others, then we would live in a much calmer world.

PAUSE

The power of pausing is my absolute favorite tool for rewiring old patterns. Pausing can be done anytime and can be as simple as taking an intentional breath. In a world where we are told to go-go-go, pausing is a potent and powerful pattern interrupt that allows us to shift our energy instantly.

I am going to invite you to take a full minute to pause right now:

• Set a timer for one minute, and pause.
• Close your eyes, if you feel comfortable.
• Take a few deep breaths, exhale fully.
• Relax your shoulders and jaw.
• Feel as your ribs expand with your inhale and contract with your exhale.

How does your body feel right now? Did the minute feel like forever, or was it a complete flash?

Notice your internal state and what happens to you when you take intentional breaths. For me, it instantly brings a feeling of calm. Please note, it doesn't always take away my anxious energy; however, it allows me to experience it with an element of peace that wasn't available before the intentional breath.

What does calm feel like to you? Spend a few more breaths here and notice your body. I notice that my eyes feel less active, my muscles relax as the tension dissolves, my heart rate slows and the chatter in my mind quiets.

A state of calm is a harmonious balance of equilibrium directly in the middle of love and fear. The bottom of the pendulum swing. A veil between two worlds.

What imagery comes to mind when you think of calm?

For me, it is always nature. Watching the river flow and the clouds pass. Observing the bright colors of the birds while listening to their songs. The setting sun over the mountain range as dusk settles on the valley. Experiencing a snowing effect as the summer winds cause the Cottonwood trees to release their pollen.

Does a state of calm exist inside your thoughts, feelings, and body? If you haven't established a practice of pausing, you might be pleasantly surprised by how quickly calmness can be created.

In fact, take a moment, close your eyes, and think about the word calm. Think of all the places you feel calm in your body. What environment makes you feel safe so you can relax? Stop here for a few minutes and experience the feeling of calm. Take a few deep breaths and open your eyes when you are ready.

I know that some of you just kept reading and said, "Yeah, I know what calm is" and assumed that it is good enough. I know what calm is too, but the experience of calm is something to rediscover continually. I, myself, just sat calmly for what ended up being three minutes and experienced calm. I had a lot of things come into my mind that wasn't calming, but once those ideas left, I started to feel calmer.

If you kept reading without a pause, practice rewiring your old habituated patterns of go-go-go right now and pause. Give yourself the gift of pausing. Allow for the calm to become present and then read on!

If you seek calm from a place of love, kindness, and compassion, you will find it. Peace and acceptance are within your own being. That unearthing of calm is rewiring your energy, building a sense of security to give space for personal fulfillment. This is freedom from Modern Fear.

The more our thoughts, feelings, and actions become calm, the more we will attract calm into our lives. This is a positive feedback loop to rewire our energy. We have a choice when it comes to our internal state of being, and just like any muscle, that feeling of calm needs to be practiced and used to grow its strength. Change your thoughts, listen to your unspoken words, and practice feeling more attuned to your internal state. Trying a new intentional practice has its own unspoken fears, "What if I am not doing it right?" "Why am I not noticing a change right away?" Remember, this is a lifelong journey, and we recommit to being on this path every time we practice rewiring our thoughts, feelings, and actions.

"Present thought determines your future reality."
Lou Tice

Pausing is a practice that will help quiet an overactive mind.

There is a lot of science out there about the power of your brain waves. You are a broadcaster; your brain waves are a measurable frequency. Just like radio waves bouncing off the moon and returning to earth so that we may listen to music, your thought frequency you output will return to you as the receiver.

The thoughts you put out into the world are your energetic karmic load. A portion of your thoughts will continue to return to you so that you may learn the lessons that you are transmitting. This will continue to happen until you learn to accept what you are putting into this world returns to you, and as a result, you have a choice on how you experience reality.

If your thoughts are filled with blame, anger, frustration, stress, sadness, worry, and disappointment, things are going to be tough. Like attracts like. Change your thoughts if you want to break the cycle of your karmic load, practice the power of pausing, and see how your world transforms!

Practice listening to your thoughts; this opens the door to the invisible prison cells of Modern Fear. As your thought process changes, so too will your feelings. As you learn to recognize your feelings and accept that you have control over the way you feel, your thoughts will naturally change as well. Thoughts and feelings work together; they support each other and are your partners in life.

Pausing allows working with the partnership between your thoughts and feelings. The intentional stillness will enable you to witness and experience the evolution of your future.

TERRIFIED EXCITED

There is an edge with rewiring Modern Fear where your heartbeat will race with excitement, and your mind will be terrified by what is next.

The veil that exists between terrified and excited is transformational and is energetically easier to connect within the practice of pausing and noticing this dynamic energy.

All transformational energy has an abundant feeling. The potential of the unknown is exciting. It stimulates your heart and can be used as an amplifier for rewiring. Excitement can build on excitement. Big dreams can feel terrifying because we become trapped in the "how." When you lean into the excitement of your dreams, it helps to ease the terrifying doubt that can surface. Vocalize the potential energy that is stored within the feeling of being excited and terrified with others. This action will breathe more life into what is next and will provide an outlet to release the terrified feelings, clearing your energy to enhance the excitement that is coming.

During my travels through Africa, we ended up at Victoria Falls for an adrenaline-filled day; bungee jumping, zip-lining, and a gorge swing. I had been looking forward to this experience because doing terrifying things allowed me to break out of my numbness and feel the energy of my own life. My fellow travelers and I talked about these activities in anticipation of the experience. The day of, I woke up ready to go! The first activity was the zip-line, and I loved it.

Then we moved on to the gorge swing at the mouth of the Batoka gorge, which includes a 250-foot free fall, followed by a 310-foot long pendulum swing. After the swinging stops, they tow the rope back up the cliff's edge as you use your feet to walk up the gorge's rock wall. Terrifying and exciting, right?

I stood on the edge of the platform, harnessed to the rope, overlooking this wide mouth of the gorge. It was stunning. My adrenaline was racing, and my mind was beginning to look for an escape. The guy asked me, "Are you ready?"

LEAH LOVELIGHT MICHAEL | 207

Rapidly shaking my head side to side, "I don't think so."

"You are never going to be," he said as he released the rope.

The heavy rope pulled me right over the edge. Two hundred fifty feet is a long free fall. At first, my adrenaline was so intense; I blacked out for a moment. Then I felt a sense of relief that I was off the platform. I watched as the ground approached quickly. There was enough time for my mind to go from blackout to excitement, questioning my sanity, enjoyment, and fear for my life. Suddenly just before the ground was within striking distance, the rope slack disappeared, and I began the pendulum swing. I could feel my heart beating out of my chest. I was elevated with pure joy and excitement that I had survived, screaming out loud and pumping my fists into the air. While at the bottom waiting to be pulled up, I was convinced I was going again; there was no doubt in my mind. Then the return to the surface started, and as I took one step at a time up the cliff's edge, my mind quickly changed as my heartbeat calmed. I became clear that I was never going to do the gorge swing again.

Within this experience, many lessons came forward. I recognized that the edge between terrified and excited creates permanent change. I was excited about this experience because it put me so close to death that it made me feel alive, and I wanted to feel a passion for living; it was still buried within me at that time. Yet, once the swing was completed, I honored that this experience was truly terrifying for me, and my being didn't need to go through it again to feel life's vibrancy. I had embodied the value of living during this swing. It was at that moment that I learned that I truly do want to be alive and that I needed to start acting in accordance with this desire and to stop destroying my life through reactionary explosions.

The ultimate goal of riding the edge is to move through to transformation eventually. When we first approach an edge of terrified excited, it is nice to push up against that edge and see how you can stretch yourself. Are you able to stay comfortable within the uncomfortable feeling of terrified? Becoming too uncomfortable can cause this momentum to stall. Move your excited energy towards the terrified, allow for the stretching lessons to come forth, and then step back and build up the excitement again. Move back towards the terrifying discomfort, see how you can ease that feeling using your excitement, and then step back again and evaluate your feelings. As you practice ebbing and flowing within this edge, the change will happen more quickly, and it will not feel forced. This transition through the edge will become a transformation within you.

With all-new adventures, which transformation is always an adventure, there is going to come a time when the mind becomes terrified, and it will battle with you, telling you all the reasons why this change is not going to work. It will try to make you believe that the "how" is too complicated and make you question what the point is. The feeling of being terrified can rise, causing you to fight with your own desires. I have literally gotten into a tug-of-war with myself while trying to convince myself for all the reasons why a specific transformation isn't worth it or why it is necessary.

The sweet spot is being able to feel a little bit of the terrified feeling while not becoming overwhelmed by it. This is best achieved by listening to your heart and comforting the mind. Feel the fear and do it anyway. Allow yourself to get wrapped up with the exciting potential. Remember, fear in a small dose is a beneficial catalyst for change. In my own experience, I have found that exciting and terrifying share the vibration of fear; they just have different frequencies.

If the transformation and change do not scare you, are you truly challenging yourself for growth? The edge of terrified excited will either support you through a transformation because it is giving your energetic field the extra juice to do that next great thing, or you will be consumed by the fear that is within the terrified mind. Our brains are designed to first and foremost keep us safe; it is our brain's number one duty. Most of our minds are lazy and will want to keep us in a content feeling, even if that feeling of content is on the lower vibrational side of the emotional spectrum.

Find the edge and play within the feeling of terrifying excitement. This rewiring tool is advanced because it is stretching your edges of feeling safe, secure, and stable. Be gentle with yourself. Start within your own being, work with your thoughts, feelings, and behaviors to calibrate your core so that it can stay centered in that sweet spot right in the middle of terrified excited, where transformation can manifest.

FROM THE MIND TO THE HEART

As humans, we are blessed with a mind and a heart. Sometimes they work together in a harmonious relationship, and at other times the mind is an absolute dictator. Modern-day society is packed with fear that puts our mind in the driver seat. The manipulation that comes from marketing is designed to make you feel scarcity or fear so that you will make a purchase. The governmental "law and order" platform works to keep us in fear of each other. As you have moved through this book, I hope you have received some tools that support you in calming your mind, so that you may more readily listen to your heart.

As we rewire our relationship with Modern Fear, we practice moving from the mind into the heart.

Working to have a conscious relationship or being actively involved with your thoughts and words will rewire the way your mind works. As my negative self-talk around shame, anger, doubt, and not deserving love dwindled, and my mind became less of a boss, I was finally able to feel into my heart. Our ego resides in our loud mind and wants to be center stage. However, in my opinion, the mind is not where the essence of our soul resides.

The heart has subtle wisdom of its own. It doesn't yell at you as the mind does. Slow down to listen to your heart to hear the ancient wisdom emerge. Pause, breathe, and put your hand on your heart. This will center you and calm your mind out of its reactionary fear response. Because you are supporting your heart, it will send signals to your brain that you are okay. The fear will begin to dissolve, and your mind will become less reactive and more rational.

I know that some of you might be thinking that this sounds a little too woo-woo. At one point, when my mind was 100% in control, I did too. I want to offer you a link to a company that has been doing scientific research on the heart since 1991. Through research, they are proving the heart is an information-processing center that is more powerful than the brain and that practicing a state of heart coherence will support brain function. In other words, the heart communicates to the brain more than the brain communicates to the heart. However, because the mind can be so loud, we think that most of our directions come from the mind. The mind has convinced us that it is the guiding superstructure. As we learn to listen to our hearts, we are rewiring the internal programming that we use to guide and support us through life, moving from the mind to the heart. There is enough information on this website to give any skeptic something to chew on along with many free resources to support you in developing a more intentional relationship with your heart. I invite you to check out their website: https://www.heartmath.org/research/

The mind is a paradoxical prison that can be your enemy or ally. When we learn to balance the direction of the mind with the wisdom of our heart, our world can transform. To bridge the mind and the heart, we get to learn to express our voice, our genius within. Dr. Wayne Dyer said, "Don't let your music die inside you." I believe he was referencing the music of our hearts as we begin to live in harmonious balance within our own being. Our mind creates the words, our heart generates feelings, and our voice gives this union of words and feelings, life.

CONNECT WITH NATURE

Before there was technology, there was the magic of nature. As kids, we played outside from sunup to sundown. I was in the woods building forts, swimming in the river, and living deep within my imagination. You couldn't keep us inside. I appreciate this part of my childhood.

My mom was so good about making sure we went for hikes, played in parks, and went to the river. She seeded my love for nature and the adventures that the outdoors provides. There was a carefree liberation when we were outside. All the worries of life disappeared as we walked through the deep woods.

Then I moved to the big city of Seattle, and I forgot about being in nature. I just admired it from afar. No matter where I have been in the world, Seattle is the most beautiful city on a sunny day. The juxtaposition of the human-made architecture, surrounded by lush green trees, sitting next to lakes, and the Puget Sound while surrounded by huge, humbling mountain ranges, is breathtaking.

Jim used to call me into his office, pretending to have something urgent. He would stand up and move to the window and ask me to have a mountain moment with him. We would stand there from our viewpoint on the 18th floor and watch as the ferries glided across the Sound and sun rays danced on the snow-capped mountains. The memories still take my breath away.

It wasn't until my traveling adventures and beginning my spiritual quest that I rediscovered nature. When I speak of spirituality, I believe that there is something greater than all of us out there. I appreciate the bridge between science and spirituality. Both hold space for the invisible forces that can't be fully explained, and yet, can be deeply explored using your curiosity and imagination.

Every naturopath, healer, shaman, or witch that I have worked with has directed me to nature. Not feeling well, go for a walk in the woods. Have too much worry, visit a tree. Frustrated, sit next to the water. Depressed, build a fire.

Nature heals.

Living in Seattle, I thought that I would be a city girl for life. I loved the convenience of eating out, shopping, and Edith, our house cleaner. There was nothing like coming home the days she visited. I never once dreamed that I would live deep in the mountainous woods until the potential of this destination became an escape plan. Going from the hustle and grind of the city to the slowness of Montana shocked my nervous system as the overextension of my do-do-do energy came to a sudden stop.

As the chaos of city life dissolved and all of my suppressed trauma and drama emerged, I would often go outside in the evening so that I could feel the northern winds rush southward down the valley. I would hold my arms out and pretend I was flying. I would allow nature to blow through me, supporting the release of what no longer served my greater good.

One day during my first fall back in Montana, I was walking around my yard. The sun was out, birds were singing, clouds floating in the sky. Summer's heat had turned spring's green to brown, yet there was a crispness to the air. I became so overwhelmed with the feeling of gratitude that I fell to my knees and wept. I finally felt safe, secure, and stable enough to fully release my energetic armor and allow the vulnerability of love to flow through me. Never had I experienced such tenderness with myself. What I experienced wasn't the feeling of love that my mind conceptualized. That moment connected my energy to the distant home that I visited during my shamanic journey in Puerto Rico.

I held my hands to my heart, raised my head to the sky, and I called out, "Thank you."

I stayed with the land for some time as I wept, physically crumbling while surrendering over all of my heartbreaks and disappointments. I held myself as the wind blew, taking with it my anger against myself and others. I listened as the singing birds made me smile, and I could hear joy in their songs.

When I finally stood up, I felt as if I was a different human. I knew nature had supported a complete transmutation of myself. I had rewired the cells within my body and the essence of my soul.

Nature has always been and always will be our continual teacher.

Look at its rich history. Our Mother Earth is one of the most nurturing yet destructive organisms alive, and we are part of her. Our bodies are her creation that we use to experience life, and when we pass, our bodies will return to her.

If you find too much chaos in your life and are feeling the burdens of stress, go to nature. The park is excellent. However, there is nothing like getting away from the city's human-made creation and surrendering to nature's comforts. This could be a secluded beach or a mountainous hike. Check-in with yourself before you get there and acknowledge how you are feeling. Then after you leave, notice how you are feeling. I promise that you will always feel better. If you want more energy points, take off your shoes, and put your bare feet upon the Earth, and pause with her; soak up her goodness.

If you are not able to get away, then you can always find a tree friend, a lesson I learned from my dear friend Penny. I have many tree friends that I love and will go to for nourishment. There is one massive leaning tree that I look at every day in my neighbor's yard. I always admire how its roots can hold and support its weight. There is a giant Ponderosa pine at the start of a trailhead that draws me to it every time as I stick my nose right into the bark and smell its sweet vanilla scent. Another favorite is Aspens; their quaking leaves will always stop me. I calmly watch them dancing in the wind and listening to their clapping.

If you live in a place with fewer trees, like city centers, then fill your home with house plants. If you think you kill plants, then you should definitely get some. A house plant is a beautiful teacher of trust and love. They rely on us to nurture them, and in return, they will give us clean air to breathe.

The more time you spend with nature, the more your energetic field will rewire to align to her vibration. When you are living in alignment with your creator's energy, it feels so good. At least I think so.

NEVER TRY NEVER KNOW

After a couple of weeks traveling through Thailand, my friend Laurie and I ended up in Koh Phi Phi to celebrate the New Year. We were doing the evening right, drinking our buckets of booze when she had decided she wanted to get her face pierced, so we went on an adventure looking for a tattoo shop.

As we walked into a parlor, I noticed on the top of the wall was the painted phrase, "Never try, never know."

Something inside of me locked onto that mantra; it felt like the Universe was giving me permission to say YES to anything that I wanted, and I ran with that liberty.

Just a few weeks prior, I had met a man on the busy streets of Bangkok, who I would fall deeply in love with and have a movie worthy love affair. We would find ourselves in exotic lands, on adventures chasing waterfalls, or on a scuba quest to find Manta Rays, and we would live under the Australian Sky together. Our journey was blessed with the mantra, "never try, never know." I will be forever grateful for this thrilling love adventure that ended not out of a lack of love, but out of complete stubbornness on both of our sides.

After years of working with this mantra, I decided to get a tattoo on my wrist to remind myself always to try. Trying is all any of us can do. The night that I received my tattoo in Seattle, I met my current partner, and the path of moving to Montana together entirely falls into "never try, never know." I couldn't be more thankful for these four words that inspire exploration. The mantra provides me an opportunity to witness and question all of my hesitations, reservation, and resistances.

What have you wanted to do that you are holding yourself back from achieving? When we take internal responsibility, rather than externally project, we rewire our energy for change. We can only change ourselves. Take responsibility as being the creators of our reality. **We as individuals are our own worst roadblocks**, primarily if we are held within Modern Fear.

I was at Kings Island, a roller-coaster theme park in Ohio, and my nephew wanted to do the flying squirrel, which means they pull you up 140 feet and let you fly through the air. I wanted to be cool, so of course, I said I would do it. Then the nerves set in. I was terrified of doing another swing; the one in Africa was enough. I looked at my nephew, and I said, "I just don't know if I can do it."

He grabbed my right arm, flipped over my wrist, and pointed directly to my tattoo. "Aunt Leah," he said while tapping his finger on the tattooed words, "never try, never know."

I looked him straight in the eye in full surrender. I knew he was right, and because he stayed focused on what he wanted, I got to fly through the air with my two favorite humans strapped to either side of me. Truly a moment in time, that was a complete gift which fear almost stole from me!

What are you not saying yes to because Modern Fear has you trapped? Can you play with this mantra, "never try, never know?" You might be pleasantly surprised by the adventures that you discover!

If never try, never know doesn't feel right for you, then perhaps another mantra will feel more aligned. A personal mantra is a powerful rewiring tool because it can act as an internal compass. My mantra has only brought me gratitude for the experiences it has created. It has allowed me to check in with my heart when my mind was a "no," and our hearts are braver than our minds.

216 | MODERN FEAR: THE INVISIBLE PRISON

SECTION 4

RECEIVE

To be given, presented with, or provided something.

"The value of a man resides in what he gives."
Albert Einstein

The Universe is an abundant energetic field. Allow space for this abundance to flow to you with ease. Surrender to the knowing that if you care for yourself and nurture yourself, you will fluidly receive because you are opening your energy to love.

Whatever you desire is waiting for you. Are you ready to fully open to self-love?

When we allow ourselves to receive, there is an expansion to our energetic field because we are connecting more intimately with Universal Source. Focus your energy to actualize the completion of your dreams. Be intentional with your thoughts, feelings, and actions. Witness as the world unfolds before you with precisely what you desire.

REMEMBER YOU ALREADY KNOW

I grew up my whole life, thinking that the answers were on the outside of me. I couldn't have been more wrong.

Life gave me many opportunities to lose myself in the circumstances. I could have become a product of the criminal system. I could have become a drug addict. I could have relived my mother's story and become a single mom of four children who had to work her butt off to make ends barely meet.

The external world that I grew up in warped my perspective of humanity. When I looked to the external world for guidance, it told me to be bigger or stronger than someone else. To disrespect others to earn respect out of fear. To manipulate those who seek support, because nothing is free and help is conditional. None of these beliefs felt right to me. These delusional survival perspectives drove me towards trying to find answers to my anger, frustration, and heartbreak outside of the environment in which I lived.

No matter what I have been through or the decisions I made because of peer pressure or spite. No matter how hard I tried to destroy my life through explosive reactions. There was something that wouldn't let me.

There has always been a drive inside of me, a yearning for something more. I was blessedly born with this fire that used to consume me because I was lost in the trauma of my mind and body. It wasn't until I started to explore my spirituality or my connection with Source that I discovered my eternal, higher self. It was then this fire started to fill me from the inside rather than consume me. This fire is my energetic force, and it is connected to Universal Source.

I went to healers, therapists, shamans, religion, and witches trying to figure out what was wrong with me so that I could be fixed.

What I discovered in working with all of these guides was that they could only take me as far as they were willing to go within themselves, and we are all on different paths. They couldn't give me what I needed; however, each of them took me bit by bit along my path of self-discovery.

In a Montana lodge, during a retreat called "Deep in the Heart," we shared a sweat lodge experience. Within the darkness and the burning fire, the journey leader held space for all of us to dig deep into ourselves to release any stagnate, depleting energy that no longer served us. Emotion after emotion boiled up, and I yelled, cried, howled like a wolf, and sang. Within the darkness and the uncomfortable heat, this ancient work's medicine permeated every cell of my being. I handed over the residual shame, anger, doubt, and frustration of my past. I let that bondage drip off me as the sweat rolled down my body. My mind begged me to leave the lodge as I curled up on the bare ground, trying to escape the heat. But the love of my soul comforted me forward. I felt during that experience, I had walked through a valley of burning fire, and when I emerged from the lodge, I looked into the distance to see a stag deer, deep in the snow, staring back at me. I took this as an omen of gentleness and new beginnings.

Later, we all sat in a circle, reflecting on what arose. That was the day I discovered that there was nothing wrong with me. I was not broken, and indeed I am a whole being. That awareness stoked my fire, and a remembering within me grew that the answers lie within. Conceptually, I already knew this because anyone on a spiritual quest will hear, "the answers lie within you." In some ways, it is cliché. However, during this weekend, an undeniably familiar feeling nourished and affirmed my inner genius. I could no longer question if I belonged, if I was whole or on the "right" path. I just knew.

What was a new discovery was that rather than knowing, I was remembering. The awareness of wholeness felt like my mind, body, and soul had been connected with the golden energy of life. My being felt like one of the beautiful, sacred restored Japanese pottery, as what I once believed to be broken was bonded with the golden healing energy.

When we are in trust with ourselves, a knowing or intuition will arise. As the external world dissolves, the inner world rises, our frequency and vibration harmonious with Source energy. Life is learning to trust and to remember that you already know the answers to your questions if you are willing to pause and listen.

Receive your inner wisdom, attune to your remembering and learn to trust what you feel. Life will move you in a more fluid journey. The lessons that we experience over and over again happen because we forget to remember we already know.

Remember who you are.

STYLE YOUR LIFE

To receive the dreams you are imagining requires a commitment to the rewiring practices that will draw that dream closer. The more we practice rewiring and taking action, the more we are recommitting to making that dream more present in our immediate future. As this becomes more of a reality, our dreams will naturally grow and morph with us as we style our lives.

One tool I touched on earlier in the book was honoring our future self and our present self. This is the same for bigger dreams, too. Where I sit right now writing this book, my present self is styling life to accommodate my future dream of being a published author. I wake up, do my morning routine, turn on my computer, and I write, morning and night, one word at a time. The editing process of digging deeper has been a humbling experience. As I get closer to the end, I can feel the excitement within me for the next step. If you are reading these words, my dream is now a reality!

It is important to notice and track that my present self is styling my life to manifest my dreams. Otherwise, I can become discouraged by the amount of time things can take. My disbelief can take over and halt my action as doubt sinks in. This is why conscious recognition and celebration are part of my every day as I style my life. Never forget that it will require parts of you to morph or let go for a new you to become present. Remember that each part of ourselves wants to live. If we are not actively aware of which part of ourselves is steering our inner leadership, we could be sabotaging our growth. The parts of us that no longer serve want to stick around, and are likely a subconscious programmed habit. It takes conscious rewiring for these parts to let go.

Our present self makes all of the daily decisions for the future. Be aware of what your thoughts, feelings, and behaviors are curating.

Stress keeps us in our reptilian brain, which focuses on safety, and prevents accessing the part of the brain where we think about the future. Safety, security, and stability must be satisfied before we can dream too far in the future. The stress of Modern Fear can make it a challenge to think about life five days from now, let alone 5-10 or 30-40 years from now.

So let's take a few steps back and recognize that the future you are considering is any moment beyond right now.

I am going to encourage you to take a moment here and imagine exactly how you want to spend your daily life without barriers or restrictions. Use your imagination and specifically design how you want to experience your lifestyle.

This process can feel intimidating. Worrying about the "how" can cause overwhelm or despair. Be gentle with yourself, and quiet your critical mind. Forget the "how" and dream.

I invite you to get comfortable, take a few deep breaths, and relax your shoulders. Open your mind, feel into your heart, and allow yourself to style your life.

Start by imagining your day, be as specific as possible.

- Does the alarm sound, or do you naturally awaken?
- As you get out of bed, what is the first thing you do?
- Are you rushed or at leisure?
- As you awaken your home, how does it feel?
- Are there projects to be accomplished, or is everything neatly put in its place?
- As you draw open the curtains, what do you see outside your window?
- Do you have a deck to enjoy the morning?
- Do you have children or animals? How are they part of your future?
- Do you leave your home for work, or is there a home office?
- When you get to work or the primary objective for the day, what are your feelings?
- Are you relaxed or stressed?
- Are you passionate about what you are about to do?
- What are you about to do? This can be anything; the future is not constructed yet, do not limit yourself by your current reality.
- Are you helping others? Are you an executive for a corporation?
- What is your passion? How do you fill your day with purpose? What matters most?

- Have you moved your body?
- Have you eaten foods that will nourish you?
- How much water have you drunk?
- When you leave work for the day, how is your commute?
- Are you in your car? What type of car is it?
- As you return home, what feelings come forward?
- As you pull up to your house, what you see?
- Where is your home located?
- Who are the people that fill your life, friends, family, or strangers, and what attributes do they contribute to your lifestyle?
- How does your evening unfold?
- Are you working on projects, sitting in front of the television, or out for dinner with people you love?
- How do you wrap up your day?
- Do you organize your life for tomorrow?
- Are you falling into bed exhausted from the events of the day?
- Laying in your bed, thinking about the day, what are you grateful for, and what are you looking forward to for tomorrow?

Now imagine beyond the day; take a look at a week, a year, or even years down the road.

- What have you accomplished?
- How many hours a week do you spend working?
- How much time do you dedicate to self-exploration and growth?
- What contributions have you made for the greater good of your community?
- What do people say about you?
- What is your legacy?
- Will your life impact those closest to you, or have you impacted your community or the global culture?

How do you feel reading and answering these questions? If you are feeling resistance within your design of these questions, perhaps you are not fully ready to receive this new life. Remember that if a part of you is holding on to the way things are habituated, then this new future is requiring internal parts of you to shift or to energetically die to make room for this new reality.

224 | MODERN FEAR: THE INVISIBLE PRISON

I am going to invite you to start a practice, set a timer for five minutes, and close your eyes, get curious with both the potential of and the resistance for these shifting energies and use your imagination for what is possible.

Your future is yet to be written. Pull out a sheet of paper and write down the dream that came forth.

The most important question you can ever ask yourself is: "How do I want to feel?" Connecting to how you want to feel is the magic sauce within this dreaming exercise. Once you feel it, it becomes real, which will reinforce the belief of possibility.

If you are imprisoned in Modern Fear, or if you feel like you do not have control of your life, it is hard to believe this question can be true or possible. If you are in a state of stress, enslaved to the debt of others, it is difficult to believe that your future can be anything that you want it to be. Remember, you get to choose how you feel, and that liberation will allow you to claim any reality that you wish to. You just have to get out of your own way. Which I know is tough; I personally still struggle with this, and I keep on trying.

Do not settle.

If you want more, open your mind and heart to that desire. The best tool for this practice is to detail your wants clearly, imagine the feelings of achieving them over and over again. Write them down, speak them out loud, record, and listen to them repeatedly.

I sit here looking out my window on a rainy spring day. The clouds are dark, the wind is blowing, and yet the birds are still singing their spring song. There was never a point in my past that I ever dreamed that the life that I am currently living was possible. I had no idea that life could be so simple and rewarding. Dream as much as you can, and your future will be even more than you can imagine.

Our ability to dream is directly connected to our past and the way we are living right now. Our future lifestyle will always be evolving. Remember to evaluate your dreams and rewrite them as life continues. Make sure to stay on track with **your** values, speak them out loud, and listen to **your** desires. Hear **your** wants and needs, and take action to achieve.

LEAH LOVELIGHT MICHAEL | 225

GIVING & RECEIVING

The concept of receiving brings up many feelings for me. On my journey to receiving, I have had to move through my feelings of worthiness and deservedness. I was programmed from a young age to believe that I didn't deserve to receive and that I must work for everything. I didn't have a source that unconditionally gave to me; everything was attached to a "price." One of the biggest injustices of low-socioeconomic communities is that the food I put in my mouth takes away from your plate, or the job I work prevents you from getting one. It is a lifestyle of scarcity, and to receive within scarcity is filled with attachment and guilt.

Receiving is beyond the material world, as we can receive emotionally as well. To receive love can also feel challenging, especially if you grew up with love attached to a condition. I was programmed to believe that abuse was love. I know with 100% certainty that my mother loves me. I am extremely grateful for her love because I know so many people question their mother's love. But, just because my mom loves me with all of her heart doesn't mean that I can receive that love. I am still breaking down those barriers around my heart.

I dream of a day when I can love my mom without being triggered. I am always having conversations with my guilt as to why I am still afraid to open up to her. I am safe. I am stable. I am secure. In reality, she can no longer impact my life, except for the fact that I know how much it would mean to her for me to open my heart and receive her love fully. This is a path I vow to continue to walk, crawl, and sometimes rest on as I discover how to learn to receive love. The magnificence of love still feels tender and scary to me, and yet I know that my purpose in life is to serve love. So I get to be gentle with myself, have uncomfortable conversations with my mom, and continue to dream of an unconditionally loving relationship with her.

Because it still feels uncomfortable for me to receive, I am actively working on aligning to this abundance frequency. In some ways receiving causes me pain, as I am still embodying my worthiness. Receiving is a practice; it is as simple as that.

Prosperity Consciousness, or abundance, follows the laws of attraction.

In the beginning of our relationship, I wondered how I could get my partner to understand how much I love him. The answer surfaced that to love him more that I must love myself more. This was an interesting awareness because it taught me that receiving starts from the inside. The more we have a feeling within us, the more we will attract it from our external world. So instead of smothering my partner, I focused my energy internally and discovered how to practice self-love so that I may receive and attract more love into my life.

What do you want more of in life? Now that you understand the impact of Modern Fear, are you able to feel these desires? Remember that fear can be a repellent and will cause you to doubt what you desire, just like my fear that I am not enough repelled my ability to feel love. Are you ready to welcome your desired blessings into your world, or are you still going to stand in your own way?

Universal Energy is in harmonious balance. If you are giving away frustration, the Universe will make sure you receive frustration. If you are giving away love, the Universe will make sure you receive love.

While our thoughts are important, it is not enough to only think about what you want to receive. You get to interact with that feeling and allow for it to grow its own life. When I dream of the future, and I think about the retreat community I want to create, I get to acknowledge the feelings of doubt that surface and support my own being moving through this doubt. I also get to play with the potential energy that emerges when I imagine sitting around a fire, sharing collective wisdom with others who are on the same path. Or walking guests into the garden to pick the vegetables they will eat for lunch so that we continue to unite and bond with nature.

When working with receiving, appreciation is the most potent magnet we can utilize. There is an entire thought philosophy around the method of Appreciative Inquiry. That which is appreciated with curious intrigue has immense value, which attracts more value. When we practice appreciation or gratitude, it is an energetic alignment that life is a gift. As we embody this value, we will naturally become more attractive, and we will be able to receive more fluidly.

Modern-day culture teaches us to give with a condition, you pay me, and I will provide this service. If I do this for you, what's in it for me? These are subconsciously supported programming messages that mass media and marketing manipulation train our brains to function within. If we look to nature as our teacher, you will never see nature holding itself back or putting conditions on its giving. The sun rises every day, the plants release their seed so that the forest can grow, and animals migrate to follow their food. Nature continuously gives, and it never hoards or holds back its energy. The more we can connect into the feeling of nature, the more quickly we will be able to drop into that universal flow of giving and receiving.

Give on the level you wish to receive. If you want more happiness, how are you demonstrating happiness in the world? If you want more money, how are you respecting your relationship with money? Energetically, to receive, you must take action in alignment with what it is you want to receive.

Our ability to receive is directly dependent upon clearly defined intentions, the quality of our attention, and the resiliency of our willpower. Being within the integrity of this alignment supports taking action and declaring to the Universe that you are ready to receive the gift of prosperity. Asking for what you want breaks through the barriers of receiving. Having faith and dedication to your desire is also pivotal to this breakthrough. To receive, we must persevere through our doubts and internal roadblocks.

When we find a harmonious flow of giving and receiving, we move into reciprocity of unconditional universal connection. Unconditionally giving is telling the universe that we are ready to receive unconditionally, and this energetic awareness is attractive.

WHAT PURPOSE DOES LOVE SERVE?

"You can't blame gravity for falling in love."
Albert Einstein

Like fear, love is an evolutionary force, an instinctual energy that causes attraction.

Evolutionarily, fear pushed us into a community for protection, and love pulled us into partnerships for reproduction. Love seeded desire for altruism, cooperation, and parental investment in children. We established supportive partnerships birthing the modern family.

It's not too complicated: fear gave us community for safety, and love gave us family for joy.

Love and fear are two feelings at the source of our emotional evolution. Our survival and joy are dependent upon having both emotions fine-tuned and in working order.

What we are facing today is an epidemic of people completely disengaged with the power of love. We are told that love is woo-woo. Modern-day mass media and manipulative marketing found in all sources of entertainment are saturating people with fear. The theatrics of how our society portrays love and fear causes confusion. As individuals, we have forgotten to pay attention to our true inner feelings because external stimuli are manipulating us.

We have forgotten that love is about a union, and fear is about survival. This has driven the individualism of humanity and has broken down the collaboration of the community.

Instead, we have locked ourselves away inside an invisible prison, resulting in the undervaluing of our personal feelings. We now look to the text of words for comfort. Who talks on the phone anymore to hear a real voice? We look to social and mainstream media for accomplishment as we share about what we have achieved or are trying to achieve. We share images of a perfect life because we are too afraid to show vulnerability. It has made an expectation of what love and life should look like, rather than how it actually feels. Love isn't about sunshine and rainbows; it is about compassion, kindness, and respect. Love is portrayed as a weak emotion when it is the grandest of them all. Love will take you to the deepest depths and the highest heights.

We are looking to technology for recognition of our existence and acceptance of who we are. To feel love, we have given the power over to external stimulation, rather than internal fostering of tenderness.

The evolution of human social interaction is mind-blowing when I look around and see how we are currently relating to each other (or rather the lack of relation to each other). People's heads are down, their attention screen-locked to devices. Walking into a restaurant, you see tables filled with people sitting across from each other, on their phones, not speaking with each other.

Cordial formalities are slipping away. People are in such a hurry; they don't hold doors anymore. Young people sit down on buses, while the pregnant and elderly stand. Pleasantries and consideration of how someone else is doing are no longer asked or spoken.

The saddest part of observing our environment is that people have lost their eagerness for curiosity. The answer has already been discovered because it is only a few clicks away. Humans are losing the capacity to problem solve without the aid of an electronic device. Astro Teller, of Google X, has demonstrated that human's ability to adapt was surpassed by the rate of technological change, which in essence means that we are culturally at a point where we rely more heavily on technology than the wisdom within, and this is a disconnection from our humanity.

You can go through life with little participation nowadays. You don't have to personally interact with anyone anymore because of the online reality that has been created. This lack of connectedness contributes to Modern Fear increasing its hold on culture because it is keeping us from the personal experience and expression of love that can only come from human connection. Love is a human emotion; it is not one that can be artificially simulated.

Love is the greatest feeling that culturally has been idealized since the beginning of time. Love takes you deep and can also make you weep.

Love makes the impossible seem probable.

Love is also a great mystery. It is incredibly difficult to define and is relative to the person experiencing it. Storytellers share tales of incorruptible virtue to explain the depths of love. These stories make you feel enlightened and are often attached to tragedy. To know love, you are promised pain. It is an inevitable outcome, and it is this knowing of future sorrow, sadness, or heartbreak that supports us in being able to feel the fullness of love. It is this bond that unites love and fear. This was my personal awakening when Jim passed; if I didn't love him so much, his passing wouldn't have been so painful, and without the pain, my love wouldn't have been able to support my transformation.

My greatest fear right now is the passing of my aging boxer, Scrappy Biff Doo. I have never known a loyalty of love more fully than his imprint on me. I lay in bed next to him lost in anticipatory grief because the day his soul leaves his body is one that I dread and know will require all of my willpower to go on. And yet, I fall in love with him more and more each day. I will not hold back my love, trapped in Modern Fear. I embrace the knowing that someday this sacred love will become my most painful journey. I vow to the bond that we share, I will go on and carry that love forever in my heart. The love will always be available to me for inspiration, laughter, and tears.

The loss of love allows you to understand its grandeur. Love is a feeling of duality; it is amplified when its vacancy follows its presence. We can curse its existence because it can hurt badly, and yet without knowing its potential pain, we might not be able to experience its full spectrum. There is a great cohesion within the feeling of love. It bridges us to the delicacy of life.

The loss of love and the pain that follows is debilitating. To me, it feels like my spirit is yanked from my being. I know this heartache from personal experience, and yet, I am still encouraging you to love more deeply. Love is the connection to our Source energy, do not let it become a barrier of fear.

Love existing results in a permanent change; you will evolve with each loss. Losing love, either through death or break-up, is an opportunity to recommit to the love of self. The power of self-healing through love is transformative.

The vacancy of love leaves a painful void, which can create an energetic vacuum that will suck you into Modern Fear. If unchecked, the critical mind will prevent the process of expressing your emotions. The only way that I have found to move through this pain is to sit with the uncomfortable feelings until that painful void is nourished with acceptance and forgiveness of the loss.

Even the idea of losing someone or something that I love is enough to build an invisible prison, breathing life into Modern Fear. The pain that can come from the idea of loss takes my breath away. It paralyzes my energy, creating desperation to hold on tighter. Conversely, it might feel easier to let go sooner. Hurt me before being hurt.

The depression that followed the loss of love changed the conversation I had with myself. Without consciously being connected to my feelings, I could have quickly fallen into the trap of negative self-talk.

- "Why did this happen?"
- "How will I go on?"
- "Why me?"
- "Am I not good enough?"
- "What did I do to deserve this?"

In comparison, rather than using negative self-talk and getting further lost in grief and depression, I practice using my energetic tools to be curious and seek out the appreciation of love.

- What lessons did I receive in life because of the presence of this love?
- How will I support the continuity of this love's energy as I share my hero's journey through this experience?
- In what ways did this love create an opportunity for me that I can continue to honor?

I give appreciation to Jim and the passing of his life every day that I walk out onto my deck and see the beauty before me. This experience does not replace Jim. If I could have him back for one more dinner party, you better believe I would jump at that chance.

Nothing is greater than feeling love. It brings a sensation of being cocooned in security that is rooted in light. When sharing love with someone, or something, I can feel their soul respond to that acknowledgment of my acceptance. Use love's dynamic energy as an amplifier to create space for greater things. The energy of love is the most powerful tool of them all. We can use it for self-compassion as we recognize all the ways we have blocked the potential of our life. We can use it when we reclaim our energy and nurture the self-love within. We can use it as we rewire our present and future self, learning to stay centered when faced with fear. Love is the doorway to receiving.

The frequency of love energy is palpable. The bond of love that is shared is also an invisible force. At its highest form, you will find unconditional love. It can be witnessed by the calmness of those experiencing its joy. When you see two friends deep in intimate conversation, that soul connection between humans is sacred to witness. Love can look many ways, from simple acts of kindness to falling head over heels. The practice of being present to love is to connect to your ability to calm your thoughts and open your heart. You can sense how love fills a space.

Love is dynamic, and I believe it exists between any interaction where you feel respect, trust, and vulnerability for someone or something. Respect, trust, and vulnerability amplifies and empowers love's frequency to grow stronger.

The idea of love is complicated; both love for others and love for self. Love is an internal state of being as well as an external experience. For so long in my life, I didn't like myself. I was lost in Modern Fear, and as an adult, I am still learning to love myself unconditionally. I honestly believe that for most of us, we will be the last person who we love unconditionally. Do you find it easier to love others or yourself?

How much do you love yourself?

How often do you stop and feel the vibrational frequency of your own love?

How often do you express self-love through your thoughts, feelings, and actions?

Our ability to receive is connected to our ability to love ourselves. The more self-love we have, the more attractive we become, and the more attractive we become, the bigger our internal magnet and the more we will receive.

Loving others is easy, it is natural, but loving ourselves - now that takes work. You know all of your secrets. You know all of your dark sides. You know what you are capable of, and yet you still get to practice being able to love yourself.

To love yourself to the fullest and purest potential, commit and recommit to yourself and the full spectrum of power that is within you. For me, this practice looks like recognizing where I am numb or not feeling. I continue to release and reclaim my energy from Modern Fear. Rewiring my frequency to be more aligned with the highest form of myself allows me to receive the abundant love of Source energy openly.

FREEDOM OF INTERNAL ALIGNMENT

As a teenager, I remember watching the movie Braveheart, the story of William Wallace. At that time, I was rebelling against social structures, creating an even more difficult life for myself than was necessary. I related so strongly to this movie because of the injustices I grew up experiencing. I had always felt oppressed and disregarded by people in power, who had all the money that controlled our society.

William Wallace was a character of his inner truth. He understood his place in society, and God willing, he hoped for more by liberating his clansman free of the injustice of tyranny. He led with outrageous enthusiasm, so much so that both his peers and his enemies revered him. This man had one truth; his soul's purpose for living was **freedom**. He believed and hoped with such devotion, that even at the end of the movie, while he was being tortured into admitting something that was not true to him, he never wavered. Even his closest friends were silently begging for him to take mercy as they watched him suffer. No one that believed in him would blame him for surrendering to end his torture. And yet, he stayed aligned and centered in his purpose. He was a leader who knew the power of holding his truth and desired the liberation of his people. He fought for what he believed in until his very last breath. I can still hear the first time I heard his exclamation of "FREEDOM." Something broke inside me, and I cried hysterically. Not because of the tragic end; no, I wept because I too wanted freedom from an invisible prison that I did not fully recognize yet. In fact, at that point in time, I was still building my walls.

Freedom is a state of being. It means that there are no barriers around us that block our energetic flow. Rather, we have healthy boundaries and can stay centered in our own being, so that we may experience the world lovingly and openly, rather than in a fearfully contracted way. Once we have found the sovereignty within our own self, we have discovered a state of freedom, an extremely attractive energy for receiving.

I hope that by this point in the book, you as a reader have become aware of the walls you have built around your feelings and that you are celebrating the hard work that you have done in breaking them down. The release from these walls gives you the gift of absolute presence.

Being here right now is the only moment that matters. The practice of presence is a tool for freedom. It keeps your energetic doors open, preventing you from being imprisoned by your past or lost in your future potential. Both can lead to inaction in the present moment.

Freedom is a practice of presence. There is nowhere else to be, there is nothing else to do, except be here in this moment.

ON THE PATH OF LIBERATION

The freedom that comes from owning, accepting, honoring, and holding love, light, and compassion is a freedom that can never be taken from you. That freedom becomes an ember of your firepower. It is your life force energy that will contribute great things to the world.

The potential of what is possible when we find the freedom of autonomy over our feelings by releasing our Self from Modern Fear is limitless. I have become sovereign, for the most part, from external stimuli that used to hold my mind, body, and soul hostage, because I am unafraid to feel my feelings.

For each person, freedom will mean something different, and the rewards that follow will be linked to your definition of freedom. For William Wallace, it was the liberation of his clan's people. For me, it is the gift of presence and being able to feel all of my feelings without the critical mind blocking the unconditional love of my heart.

Spend some time and contemplate these questions: What are the rewards to your freedom and liberation from Modern Fear? What might be possible if you have a loving relationship with your fears rather than resisting them?

When facing a task, do not think of the difficulty; think about the reward that follows.

For example, in early January, I committed to getting into shape and signed up for a new gym membership, hitting it hard. This New Year's resolution behavior is an attempt to rewire previously ingrained patterns.

The gym can be an intimidating space filled with nerves and unfamiliarity. Beginning a new workout routine hurts. Muscles get sore! Pain has been a symptom that encouraged me to take a break or stop a newly-formed behavior. I know that being physically active will help me to feel better and lose weight. I know where I physically want to be, but I have used the excuse of pain to become trapped in the transitional period of change.

Other distractions can discourage the gym. With the pain being acknowledged, these other interferences become even louder. Going to the gym takes too long. I feel self-conscious. My body hurts, and I do not know how to use different machines. So I skip a day.

My attention becomes disconnected from the intention of feeling and looking better. I lose focus on the reward of the gym and get lost in the task of the gym.

To receive rewards when developing a new habit requires a clear intention, focused attention, direct action, and willpower to push through the unseen fear of transition.

What would happen if you focused on the rewards of the gym rather than the side effects?

Your clothes are fitting better; your mile run has improved by 20 seconds, you have a new social outlet, not to mention the excellent eye candy at the gym. Whatever the reward is for you, let this be your focus, not the actual task.

Celebration is an amplifier for freedom. Focus on the reward. As you achieve milestones, acknowledge your success. Tell yourself, "good job." **Find a way to celebrate even the smallest success.**

Rejoice in your hard work. Do not waste your time focusing on the little failures and beating yourself up for not meeting your expectations.

Again, we are the only species known to repeatedly beat ourselves up for the same "mistake." Nature does not act in this way. It learns, adapts, and moves forward; otherwise, it dies.

Life is a constant practice. You will succeed, and you will fail. You get to decide which feeling you want to support and grow.

The celebration of freedom, whether it is societal, physical, or emotional, is the ultimate reward.

THE FUTURE

The final frontier.

The future is limited by one thing: lack of, or an unwillingness for, imagination. Imagination can take you anywhere. However, if you are trapped in Modern Fear, you might not be able to access the full potential of your imagination because that part of your brain is being blocked by the stress response of the primal or reptilian brain.

In general, society tells us that we can be anything we want to be within the constructs of its funnel. Our parents encourage us to think about the great things we want to be in the future. The generations of the past advocate for your future based on their own experiences.

The future knows that you are coming. Your heart's desires can take many forms, and you are the leader of your own path.

In the fourth grade, I told my mom I wanted to be a heart doctor. I asked for a model heart to figure out how it worked. I remember looking at an encyclopedia to learn as much as I could about the heart. I was obsessed with the potential energy and excitement. In my mind, there was no way the dream of becoming a heart doctor wasn't a possibility.

Thirty years later, I still dream of being a heart doctor. The difference is now I facilitate healing and supporting the heart's energy. Though my heart's desire is taking a different form, it is still evidence that I have always been on this path.

Without pausing to feel and to hear the beating of your heart, your imagination will only take you so far.

Your own heartbeat never lies to you. It is an instant truth; the heart never sugar coats anything. In contrast, the mind buffers to protect us from potential fear, which narrows our scope of imagination. When you want to know if your future is going to be "good," you will not have to wonder if you learn to feel and listen to your heart.

Where you end up in life is dependent upon your outlook. The most important perspective to hold is the future you want to receive while honoring your present feelings. When you worry about things that are beyond your control, it brings on anxiety and doubt. These feelings limit your belief. They dampen or confuse your imagination. Both can trick you into believing your hopes are impossible.

Fear can consume your attention, and it can put itself in front of love. This is when your future becomes tough.

Fear will attract more fear, and before you know it, you are imprisoned by Modern Fear.

Reactive anxiety and doubt that originate from Modern Fear control your capacity to have positive memories, limiting your imagination because stress prevents your brain from being able to think too far in the future.

To experience your future with an open heart is the receiving of your most dynamic and impactful future possible.

Unlike in the past, the future has no absolute elements. There is no limit to how great or how bad it can be. You can hope for its greatness. But if less than ideal events happen along the way, well, that's life. We learn, adapt, and grow by establishing a practice of working with the healing tools that have been shared throughout this book. Difficult things won't hold you down!

Or you can have reactive anxiety about the uncertainty and doubt the outcome of its greatness, and when tough stuff happens, you can let it bring you down.

The path you choose is up to you.

In truth, we are always receiving what life has to offer. The offer of life is a direct reflection of your internal state of being. If you don't like the reality you are receiving, then it is time to do some inner work focusing on your thoughts, feelings, and actions.

LOVE IN ACTION THROUGH COMMUNITY

In theory, the future is purely unlimited possibilities. By applying the law of attraction, you know that present thought determines your future reality. Set your intentions, dream big, hope for your desired future, and open your heart to receiving this bountiful gift.

The more you seek unconditional, life-giving love for yourself and others, the more love will come into your life.

Loving yourself more increases the capacity to love others more. Self-love is a conduit for a greater love that is aligned in the greater good.

Love brings with it acceptance. When we feel love for something, we accept it for what it is. It calms our heart rate. It brings a sense of balance and simplified peace to the experience.

Love from our community eases and supports the transitions into our future life. On the journey to becoming the published author of Modern Fear, I leaned into the love of my community for belief and inspiration when I doubted my ability. I worked with my dear friend Sara to dig deeper into my stories that I held back from sharing because I was afraid. It was truly her love and support that allowed me to trust being able to go deeper into this journey.

Love is a feeling that grows with sharing. **It feels good to feel loved, and it feels even better when you can feel your own love.**

Thinking about getting love rather than giving love can lead to an imbalance of love. The ego becomes the driver of love and ultimately forgets that other people need love too. The hope in love can fade away.

When we are in a loving community, love is always being reflected to you. This was a vital part of my own journey through the house of mirrors. The moment that I recognized that the love of my community was a reflection of the love I was giving to it was a humbling and sacred moment for me. It allowed me to witness what my love felt like, which allowed me to feel my love internally and undeniably.

In theory, when you think of your future, you also should be thinking about the other people in your life's future as well. Love cannot exist on its own. Nothing can.

Every choice you make will change your world, rippling out to the people that are part of your life. No one person is an island. We are always connected. Community is about respecting the ecosystem of life's collaboration.

Every time you feel love for others, your world grows more beautiful. Conversely, when you feel fear of others, your world grows rougher.

When we are in a loving community, we are in a safe space to be able to share all of our feelings and for them to be heard with an open heart and not a critical mind. Remember the rewiring tool and practice listening to your heart's guidance towards love.

Your heart is your magnetic north in finding your path through life. Let love be your compass for receiving the community that nourishes you.

DO WHAT MATTERS

I believe that we are all souls having a human experience. I believe that this human body is a momentary pause in the perpetuation of our energy. Energy can never be destroyed. It can only be transmuted or transformed.

Our bodies are the soil of this Earth. When we pass away, these sacred vessels will disintegrate and return to the life cycle of Mama Gaia. Our souls are our spiritual body, and they will return to their Source as well.

The time we have on Earth is a false illusion. It feels so damn real, and yet in the cosmic timeline, it is a fraction, of a fraction, of a fraction of time.

If we are lucky, we will get many years to walk upon these fertile lands. **Life is a gift** that we either get to unwrap with enthusiasm every day or squander in our suffering. That choice is up to you. If you remain trapped in Modern Fear, life might be the gift that is not received, as the illusion of fear prevents fully living.

What matters most to you? What is the hierarchy of your value system? Does your reality reflect these feelings?

Your life is absolutely unique to you and what matters most to you is an individual experience. Do what matters to you with your life. Don't let the external noise dictate your roadmap. Only you know what is truly important to you during this journey. The answers are within you.

Once my reality changed to living in a mountainous valley along a river called Rock Creek, I quickly understood that if I melted away, life will go on. It is incredibly humbling to acknowledge the insignificance of my life and yet how unique and powerful my own expression is. My life matters most to me, which was an uncomfortable realization that my journey required me to go through. This realization was the missing piece of the puzzle for me to stop seeking external validation for my actions and to start allowing myself to do what matters most for me.

Life is a perpetual energy and force multiplier. It lives through us and nature. It is a consciousness of its own. Celebrate it and do what matters most in alignment with the greater good and you will live in a magical world, I promise.

PAST, PRESENT, FUTURE

You cannot have a future if you do not have a past, and you cannot have a past without having the present. When you are too far in the future, it is like running on a treadmill: lots of work, and only a number to tell you how far you've gone. If you are stuck too far in the past, it is like moving in and out of solitary confinement within your invisible prison. The moment you get released, you will end up in solitary again because you are looking backward and getting trapped in the same story.

The past Self has many stories and experiences filled with feelings that are still being carried in the body today. The future self is awesome because it does not have the baggage of the past unless you are lost in worry. Both can be used as an escape from your current reality, which is also known as the present.

To live in the present is purely practice. It can feel hard to stay present because the future is so endless, and the past is weighted and real; be kind to yourself in this practice.

To be in this moment, in these words, in this room, in this body, in this life, in this interaction, to be present to all things now is really dang hard. I still want to escape from time to time. We are human, we love to be comfortable, and yet, I know the real richness in life is right now.

So we get to be present to our attention and where it is directed. Is it in this moment? Is it in the past? Or is it in the future?

When we spend too much time in the past, your present looks and feels a lot like your past. Your past self is not allowing your present self to be. **Who do you want to be? The person you once were or the person you are now?**

Depending on who you want to be is where you direct your attention.

If you direct your attention too far into the future, it takes away from the now. This moment in time is the only one that is real. It is important to be consciously aware of your reality.

Then there are those magical moments, where the **Future Self** is present to receive the gifts of the **Past Self**, and the **Present Self** is here to bear witness and facilitate the exchange. It is this very moment in time that healing happens. This is the moment in time that your quantum fields can change your current reality. I have longed for a future that is free of pain for most of my life, and to free myself of suffering, I had to be willing to be present with the pain of my past. My present self had to feel all the fear connected to that suffering to release myself from the invisible prison of Modern Fear so that my future self could live beyond the pain. This connection of past, present, and future is where my story lives. It is the magic of curiosity and the ability to pause.

This practice is where we find the wormholes for dimensional healing and our most impactful moments of the sovereignty of Self. We hold space for ourselves to transform truly.

CHOICE

L ife happens and repeats in cycles. Every time a cycle repeats, we have a choice to recognize the reoccurrence of the cycle so that we can reclaim the energy attached to that cycle. Only then are we able to continue to rewire our energetics to align with what it is we desire to receive in the future.

I have made a choice in my life to move from the suffering of Modern Fear and to allow myself to feel the liberation of all of my feelings. I chose to move through life in the light of love rather than the shadow of fear.

You have a choice to walk the line between your present self, the reflection of your memories, and the hope for your unlimited future potential.

You have a choice to allow yourself to be free of judgment, free of Modern Fear, so that you may hear and feel your inner truth or wisdom.

Your life is a direct result of the choices you made based on your thoughts, feelings, and actions. If you do not like where you are today and if you do not like what your tomorrow appears to be, then you have a choice to change and a responsibility to yourself to take action.

You can choose to listen with patience for your truth that will ultimately guide you to freedom, or you can react to fear and find yourself inside of an invisible prison. Receiving is on the other side of these choices, and now is the perfect time to choose.

Liberation, sovereignty, and joy are your choice.

ACKNOWLEDGMENT & APPRECIATION

I first would like to thank you, the reader, for your support and for going on this journey. These words are written for you to inspire love and transformation in your world.

I would like to thank my mother. I would not be the woman I am today if it was not for her. My strengths, resiliency, sense of adventure, and compassion for life are because of the way I was raised by her. It was through her influence of my upbringing I was able to discover my path out of fear. Thank you, mom, for always loving me.

There have been many people who have supported me along my journey of writing this book that I would like to acknowledge. The first is T. Ellery Hodges, author of The Never Hero Chronicles. Long before the book was ready to be published, he was the first person to help edit this book and gifted me with the title Modern Fear – The Invisible Prison. Thank you to both Penny Love and Melissa McClintock, who supported the editing process well before the message was ready to be birthed when I was still trying to force its completion. Sara Roberts, Jessica Morrison, and Erin Crabtree thank you from the bottom of my heart for your support of getting this book finished and released into the world! Alisa Heinitz, with Peak Marketing Design, thank you for the formatting and being so available as I moved to the finish line of releasing this book. Jenna Nord, thank you for your stunning photography and your devotion to being love. I also want to thank Nicholas Beuthien for the artistic creation on the cover and his partnership in life.

To the unsung superheroes and guardian angels in my life who have supported me along the way, thank you. Doris & Jim, for your love, when I was a small child. Mr. Adcock, my fifth-grade teacher. To the Sturgis family for allowing me to experience safety, security, and stability in the eighth grade. To my probation officer, Mike McLean, for seeing hope for me in my troubled youth. To my Aunt Mindy for being a teacher of compassion, long before I understood its power. Kate Houlihan, who sheltered me as

I escaped abuse. To Laurie Rumball, a friend that I know will always be there. To Jim and Melanie Currier for inspiring me to live more boldly and more kindly. To Tavish, Simara, and Izabett, three humans that give me the purpose to always try harder at being a better human. Finally, every person who has believed in me when I doubted myself. I am truly blessed to have a life filled with an abundance of unconditional love.

I want to thank Gina Roberts, Traci Carman, and all of the other beautiful humans who consistently ask about the completion of this book. It was truly because of your inquiry that I knew that I needed to keep going.

Lastly, I want to thank those that have chosen to carry the karmic load for the trespasses they brought into my life. The harm you have caused is being transmuted through the healing of my energy. I appreciate your energetic contribution to my existence and the strength that I have discovered within myself. I truly hope that you find forgiveness within yourself and be released from the bondage of suffering.

May life bring each and every one of you many blessings filled with joy and wisdom.

ABOUT LEAH LOVELIGHT

Leah Lovelight Michael is the founder of Lovelight Way, a co-creator of REVEAL Retreats, Dream Doula, and a soulFULL teacher for changemakers, soul seekers, intuitive curious, and heart-centered leaders. She is a certified XCHANGE Guide, writer, reiki master, and craniosacral therapist.

Leah is a world traveler and currently resides in the woods of Montana, where she lives with her partner Nicholas and their two boxers, Scrappy and Zoe. Leah has always been a student of life, a connoisseur of people, and a leader in self-discovery. She has moved out of her fear prison and has elevated her vibration into the embodiment of love. Her mission in life is to support those who are ready to release themselves from suffering, and she believes that this change starts within.

To find additional information and a free online course go to:
Website: www.lovelightway.com
Instagram: @leahlovelight & @modernfear
Facebook: https://www.facebook.com/modernfear

WHAT PEOPLE SAY ABOUT WORKING WITH LEAH

Rachelle Niemann,

Author of *Breaking Free From the Hustle for Worthiness*

"Working with Leah Lovelight Michael was a beautiful experience. Most of my healing work involves painful processing and realizations, but it was different working with Leah. She guided me to embrace the light and love and to connect with my truest self. She made my spiritual energy accessible and available, and things we worked on came effortlessly when I opened up to them. I'm not saying she didn't challenge me and my limitations, she certainly pushed my boundaries, but it was done with such love and gentleness that it was easy to be guided there. I have not experienced the level of ease and support that she creates anywhere else. She definitely opened my being to my spiritual energy, and I can't wait to work with her again."

Nicholas Fury,

Founder of Flow Performance Coaching

"Not sure where to begin this. The story of my connection to Leah is long, dense, and profound!

I remember hanging out with her one evening in Seattle at Starbucks. We were chatting casually when the conversation deepened, and in a moment, years of pain and fear poured out of me like a tidal wave. I'll never forget that night. Up to that point in my life, I felt pretty good about where I had been, and where I was going. Only to realize how much pent up negative energy, fear, and trauma I had been lugging around like a pile of rocks strapped to my back. Back story, my childhood, and up until a few years before meeting Leah was rough. Like kick your ass and make you wanna give the fuck up rough. After our conversation, I was a bit confused but filled with an amazing euphoric sense of relief and liberation. Like something permanently changed in me for the better. I now know this is called an emotional release. That night through

Leah's guidance and empathy, I was able to let go of an immense amount of pain. Pain that never came back. I'm not sure where I heard this, maybe it was Leah, but in those moments of healing, we learn how to set down baggage that isn't serving us anymore and back to the universe it goes.

After that night, I would continue to refer to Leah during times of confusion and chaos in my life. And rightly so, as I endured years of trauma, that trauma would take years to resolve and heal. There were more intense moments in our conversations after that first night but slowly over time, they became less and less. She has been a great mentor and guide in my life! I have tools now that I didn't before and continue growing with self-sufficiency. One of the biggest things I've learned from Leah is self-love! Self-love can take you anywhere.

Up until discovering self-love, I vaguely remember ever having experienced more than fleeting moments of joy in my life. Pretty crazy.

Over the years, I've encountered other people, friends, coworkers, and such that had expressed or shown signs of being trapped by the garbage in their pasts, searching for guidance and a way out. Hearing their stories, I shared with them mine and the people that helped me along the way. I've put them in touch with Leah, and every time she finds a way with them.

The gratitude I have for Leah, and our time together is immense. She's a super woman with superpowers!"

Penny Love

"Leah has taught me about showing up for people I love, unconditionally. Even the ones who have hurt me. Learning about unconditional love, forgiveness, and intentional hugs are a few of the blessings Leah has added to my life. One thing that Leah has, and very few people I've ever met have is the most powerful hug. They are strong and mighty. She commits to the hug in a way no one else does. She won't settle for weak hugs or short ones. She is intentional and stands in the hug-field for the time necessary.

I will never forget the spiritual experience I shared while Leah was holding space and guiding the healing session. A bird, we think it was a finch, showed up on the bird feeder. Its colors were so vibrant it didn't seem real. I had a sense it was my grandmother visiting me in Spirit form. I asked what the message was and heard, "show me, love." As I said it aloud, immediately, her dogs started wagging their tails and came over to me and started licking me. I burst out into tears, then I asked Leah for a hug, and when she hugged me, I felt my grandmother in my arms. It was the most intense, electric, and powerful moment I've ever experienced before. Afterward, Leah said she felt my grandmother come through her. That was such a powerful exchange of love, spirit, and unconditional love through her hug. I will forever be grateful to Leah. Thank you! I love you."

Jessica Morrison,
Founder & Creator of HulaHealing

"From the moment I met Leah retrieving my coat from the chair she was sitting on three years ago, she has helped me completely transform my life. Through one-on-one support, Leah guided me out of my mind, into my heart. The accepting and safe energetic space she created allowed me to crack wide open and feel joy like I never have before. She has taught me how to truly feel life, to pause and say thank you to my lungs for breathing and my heart for beating.

During her facilitation of the 2019 Lovelight Way Retreat, Leah gave me the opportunity to walk through what I consider my biggest fear in life. By asking me to lead a group hula hooping workshop, I was able to shed my fears of "not good enough" and "not ready yet" and to see that my dream of HulaHealing was already real. Leah's intuitive nature and strength opened the door so that I could walk through my own modern fear. Since starting my business, Leah has continued to cheer me along every step of the way.

She is vivacious, strong, grounded, playful, dedicated, and is truly of love and light. Leah has an undeniable ability to hold you in your highest frequency and potential, no matter how afraid you may be. Her sight of your most incredible life is clear, and she has the passion and magic to help pull you there and lovingly call out your resistance along the way.

I am eternally grateful for Leah Lovelight Michael and the pillar her work and support has created in my life."

Beverly Chaney

"It is truly an honor and privilege to witness Leah share her Lovelight way of releasing Modern Fear with the world. Why, you ask? Because having the awareness and ability to release fear saved my life...literally. The most incredible gift I received from The Lovelight Way was gaining the full belief and understanding that everything I need is inside of ME. Leah gifted me with many tools to be able to release fear and align with my truth. These tools enabled me to "quiet the noise" that had ruled my existence for far too long and decipher between whether or not my thoughts, ideals, dreams, etc. were mine, imposed on me, or just borrowed along the way from my 43 years of life. The tools I learned from Leah helped me to release the things that I now know were projections from others and helped me to support others, but not take on their stories/issues. Leah also taught me how to get to a clearer and deeper understanding of who I am, what I feel, and how I feel about what I feel. Once I get to this state, I then get to decide if I want to hold onto that feeling/thought/belief or release it from my being. I now live in my power and choose how I get to live my life. I am grateful, always, in all ways. Thank You, Leah!"

Erin Crabtree

"Working with Leah shone a light on my own Modern Fear, and inspired me to begin the process of breaking through the armor surrounding my heart. Leah offers the Truth in such a loving and unwavering way; my Soul sang in recognition and my Ego was exposed, a necessary unveiling for vital healing and expansive growth. Allow this book to guide your heart in breaking wide open, so that you may live the life you deserve. Thank you, Leah, for being a warrior of love!"

Made in the USA
Las Vegas, NV
10 February 2021